Herb and Spice Cookery

Monica Mawson

HAMLYN

LONDON · NEW YORK · SYDNEY · TORONTO

Contents

First published under the title 'Hamlyn's Guide
to Herbs and Spices' in 1970 by
The Hamlyn Publishing Group Limited
London · New York · Sydney · Toronto
Hamlyn House, Feltham, Middlesex, England
Second edition published in 1972
© Copyright The Hamlyn Publishing Group Limited 1972
ISBN 0 600 34384 7
Printed by Litografia A. Romero S.A.,
Santa Cruz de Tenerife (Spain)

Illustrations by Rosemary Aldridge

Foreword

ACKNOWLEDGEMENTS

The author and publishers would like to thank the following for their help and cooperation in supplying colour pictures for this book:

American Rice Council: pages 34 and 49
Argentine Beef Bureau: page 52
Cadbury Schweppes Foods Limited: page 38
Grand Marnier: pages 42 and 61
Guernsey Tomato Marketing Board: pages 42 and 52
Arthur Guinness Son and Company Limited: pages 56 and 61
Pasta Foods Limited: page 64
Sutton and Sons Limited, Reading: page 34

The subject of Herbs and Spices is so often taken for granted, but only a little thought is required to realise that the selection and addition of these many subtle flavours supply the individuality which cooking must possess.

After all, the thousands of available recipes are only guide lines. The judicious addition of herbs and spices stamps an original image upon dishes, not only of your own creation but also most important when dealing with all the stereotyped convenience foods of today.

Their ability to offer you such a wide range of variation is also coupled with another wonderful attribute – they are in themselves great space savers. They take little shelf room in your kitchen, and need only minute growing areas in your garden or window box.

My research into this fascinating subject was a revelation in itself. For today, we are indebted to some of our Roman invaders who had the time to spare from their battle training, to have the fore-thought to bring over many of the herbs which we now enjoy. Some can still be found growing wild in our countryside – chervil, fennel, oregano, and sweet cicely, to mention but a few – and remain as silent sentinels to the romance and history of our country.

The intrepid explorer, Marco Polo, following the Roman pattern, was the first man to set Europe afire with desires for the spices of the East, then commanding fantastic sums in the West – and hence to these islands.

Believe me, 'herbs and spices' are indeed our friends, and we are grateful to them for the immense variety they so readily create.

Get to know them more intimately, for they are all intriguing and will give you more and more joy.

MONICA MAWSON

Useful Facts and Figures

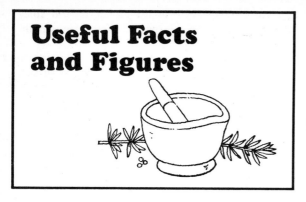

Liquid measures

6 tablespoons (4 fl. oz.)	125 ml.
8 tablespoons (5 fl. oz. or $\frac{1}{4}$ pint)	150 ml.
$\frac{1}{2}$ pint (10 fl. oz.)	275 ml.
$\frac{3}{4}$ pint (15 fl. oz.)	425 ml.
1 pint (20 fl. oz.)	575 ml.

I have worked out a plan for converting recipes from British measures to their approximate metric equivalents. For ease of measuring we recommend that solids and liquids should be taken to the nearest number of grammes and millilitres which is divisible by 25. If the nearest unit of 25 gives scant measure the liquid content in a recipe must also be reduced. For example, by looking at the chart below you will see that 1 oz. is 28 g. to the nearest whole figure but it is only 25 g. when rounded off to the nearest number which can be divided by 25.

Oven temperature chart

	Fahrenheit	Celcius	Gas Mark
Very cool	225	110	$\frac{1}{4}$
	250	130	$\frac{1}{2}$
Cool	275	140	1
	300	150	2
Moderate	325	170	3
	350	180	4
Moderately hot	375	190	5
	400	200	6
Hot	425	220	7
	450	230	8
Very hot	475	240	9

The Celcius (formerly Centigrade) equivalents are the temperatures recommended by the Electricity Council.

Ounces	Approx. g. and ml. to the nearest whole figure	Approx. to the nearest unit of 25
1	28	25
2	57	50
3	85	75
4	113	125
5	142	150
6	170	175
7	198	200
8	226	225
9	255	250
10	283	275
11	311	300
12	340	350
13	368	375
14	396	400
15	428	425
16	456	450
17	484	475
18	512	500
19	541	550
20	569	575

NOTE: When converting quantities over 20 oz. first add the appropriate figures in the column giving the nearest whole number of grammes, *not* those given to the nearest unit of 25, then adjust to the nearest unit of 25.

Notes for American users

The following list gives American equivalents or substitutes for some terms used in the book:

BRITISH	AMERICAN
Baked/unbaked pastry case	Baked/unbaked pie shell
Baking tin	Baking pan
Baking tray	Baking sheet
Base	Bottom
Cocktail stick	Wooden toothpick
Cake mixture	Batter
Deep cake tin	Spring form pan
Frying pan	Skillet
Greaseproof paper	Wax paper
Grill	Broil/Broiler
Kitchen paper	Paper towels
Mixer/Liquidizer	Mixer/Blender
Muslin	Cheesecloth
Pastry cutters	Cookie cutters
Patty tins	Muffin pans/cups
Piping tube	Nozzle/tip
Piping bag	Pastry bag
Pudding basin	Pudding mold/ovenproof bowl
Sandwich tin	Layer cake pan
Stoned	Pitted
Top and tail gooseberries	Clean gooseberries
Whisk	Whip/beat

NOTE: The British pint is 20 fluid ounces as opposed to the American pint which is 16 fluid ounces.

Introduction

The 'spice of life' is a term we use when we want to convey something exciting, something romantic. Spices, and their often associated violent history down the ages, cause a subconscious quickening of the pulses at the very thought of those far away adventures.

Archaeologists believe that the knowledge of seasoning food extends back at least 50,000 years. But the first known reference to spices was chiselled into stone tablets 5000 years ago by the Assyrians, in their version of the Creation.

Primitive man probably discovered that the taste of herbs and spices was good by the usual method: by mistake. What more likely than that he wrapped a piece of food, possibly meat or fish, in a leaf of some kind to save it from becoming burned and dusty on an open fire, and then found that the meat tasted particularly good? From that it would be but a short step to experimenting with different flavours, for the express purpose of disguising strong tasting and sometimes almost inedible items of food which often constituted their diet.

Originally, too, man depended upon plants for medicine. Without our sophisticated medical knowledge to help him, he found nevertheless that certain plants and herbs had healing properties, and he used them for this purpose.

Hippocrates, for example, the 'Father of Medicine' as he is called (4th century B.C.) left a list of hundreds of herbs which he used medicinally, many of which are still in use today.

As man progressed in knowledge, he killed off animals during the winter and salted the carcases to preserve them. Later on the salted and pickled meat needed enlivening with something: the attractive flavours of herbs and spices must have been a boon.

Then Lent used to be observed with great severity and, in mediaeval times, housewives cleared their larders of all meats, fats, eggs, oil and sweet things. Hence, pancakes on Shrove Tuesday to finish up all the good things before the great forty days fast. Only fish was allowed during Lent, and for the great majority of the populace that meant salt cod and salt herrings only.

As even eggs were forbidden, herbs and spices played a great part in the sauces to brighten this otherwise dull diet.

And these, of course, were the prime reasons why herbs and spices were used in cooking with such abandon in succeeding centuries – until refrigeration was invented to keep food in good condition, and the religious laws became less stringent.

History

The place occupied in history by herbs and spices is fascinating. The Bible contains many references to them. Amongst others it tells us that eighteen centuries before Christ, Joseph was sold by his brothers to Ishmaelite merchants carrying spices from the East. And the infant Jesus as He lay in His manger in Bethlehem was brought gold, frankincense and myrrh, by the Wise Men.

The ancient Greeks evidently thought so much of spices and herbs that they even had murals depicting saffron gatherers on the walls of the great Minoan palace of Knossos in Crete.

Then the legendary Queen of Sheba when she visited King Solomon in about 1000 B.C. took, as her principal gifts, 'camels that bare spices'. The wiser-than-all kings, King Solomon, is also thought to have amassed part of his great wealth from trading in spices. At least by an agreement with the Phoenician King, Hiram, his specially built ships carried the Phoenicians on their quests for these precious cargoes.

Later the Romans, who went first to Britain in 55 and 54 B.C. before conquering the country in A.D. 43, are said to have taken with them some four hundred varieties of herbs and spices which they planted for their own pleasure.

And when Alaric and the Visigoths sacked and subjugated Rome in A.D. 410, he demanded three thousand pounds of peppercorns as part of his price for sparing the lives of the inhabitants!

At the end of the sixth century a new prophet, Mohammed, was born in Mecca. He later married a rich widow whose wealth came from the spice trade, and thereafter for several hundreds of years the Moslems enjoyed a complete monopoly of the spice trade; keeping secret the sources from whence they came, by telling stories of incredible dangers and hardships encountered upon the route.

It was Marco Polo in the late thirteenth century, who first brought to Europe the glamorous tales of the spices in the Far East, then commanding fantastic sums in Europe, that led to the struggle for control of these rich lands. Many a slave was bought and sold for the price of a few handfuls of peppercorns; the cost of a handful of cloves was as much as a whole year's wages of a labourer; and a pound of mace bought three sheep or half a cow!

Spices also had an indirect bearing upon the building of the British Navy, since in that era they were one of the most valuable commodities for trading, together with sugar, tea, coffee and salt.

For centuries the British Isles were belaboured by marauding Vikings, the first men to build strong sea-going ships, who also invaded Spain and Portugal besides many other countries. To beat them off, the British, the Spaniards, and the Portuguese seem to have been the quickest off the mark in learning the art of how to build larger ships. With these ships, trading commenced to far distant lands for the riches they could gather. And to protect its own shipping (not to mention being able to pinch some valuable prizes on the way!) each nation began to build fighting ships, and so build up a Navy.

The Middle Ages saw intrepid explorers like Vasco da Gama, Christopher Columbus, Magellan, and later Captain Cook roaming the seas to find new lands and new wealth. They transported back to Europe, to the joy of their monarchs and the exchequers of their countries, valuable cargoes of spices and sugar (Columbus actually took some sugar canes to the Caribbean island of Santo Domingo, where he found it grew better than anywhere else in the world and it became known as 'White Gold').

Queen Elizabeth I granted a charter for the purpose of spice trading with the East Indies to a number of merchants who became known as the East India Company. On their first voyage they successfully exchanged gold, silver and mirrors for a cargo of peppercorns and cloves; so valuable that the dockers who unloaded the ships in London were given suits without pockets to stop them from pilfering the peppercorns!

The Queen was often depicted carrying a pomander, as was also Cardinal Wolsey. These pomanders consisted of an orange stuck with cloves and cinnamon bark. They were much in vogue as something that society people held to their noses when obliged to come into close contact with the poor, who often smelled unpleasantly. The price of these spices naturally enhanced the value of such a habit amongst the fashionable set.

The first pure food law in history was passed in England in 1447 – to prevent adulteration of spices!

With the discovery of Central America and the Caribbean, new spices were added to the trade, particularly cayenne, paprika and allspice. Some of these, notably paprika, became extremely popular in Europe.

America benefitted from the spice trade in another way as well. In the late seventeenth century, a young Bostonian by the name of Elihu Yale worked in England as a clerk for the British East India Company, which held a monopoly on all trade with India and whose ships brought the first cargo of cinnamon from the Moluccas.

Elihu Yale learned much from his employers about trade with the Far East, took his chances and subsequently became Governor of Madras in South India. Having made a vast fortune, he endowed what is now the Yale University in Connecticut.

To illustrate the quantity and manner in which spices and herbs were used in past centuries, here is a recipe from a fifteenth-century cookery book. The original was written in 1429. I have translated it as literally as possible into readable English, as follows:

A Rabbit, Hen, or Mallard. 'Take cony, hen, or mallard, and roast him almost enough; or else chop him, and fry him in fresh grease; and fry onions minced, and cast all together into a pot, and cast there-to fresh broth and half wine; cast there-to Cloves, Mace, Powder of Pepper, Cinnamon; then steep fair bread with the same broth and draw it through a strainer with vinegar. And when it has well boiled, cast the liquor there-to, and powdered Ginger, and vinegar, and season it up; And then thou shall serve it forth.'

And a few centuries later, here is another splendid example taken from 'The Cook's and Confectioner's Dictionary: Or, The Accomplish'd Housewife's Companion' by John Nott, 'late Cook to his Grace the Duke of Bolton', first published in 1723.

To collar and fouce PORK. 'Take a Piece of Pork out of the Side, lay it in Water all Night, and fqueeze out the Blood, then feason with Sage, Parfley, Thyme and fweet Marjoram; then cut Slices of a Leg of Veal, hack them with a Knife, and feafon them with Salt, Pepper, Nutmeg and Mace; then with your Pork on the Infide with Yolks of eggs, and the outfide of your Veal with the fame, and lay it with the Pork; then strew on the remaining Part of your Seafoning, roll it up hard into a Collar, bind it with Tape, boil it; and when it is boil'd fouce it in the fame Liquor with beaten Pepper and Ginger, and a little Vinegar. When you ferve it up, ftick the Pork with Bay-leaves or Rofemary and Flowers, and garnifh your Difh with Sage and Flowers.'

From these examples it is clear that much importance was attached to the lavish use of herbs and spices to make all kinds of meat palatable.

Since the introduction of refrigeration in Britain, however, it has been possible to enjoy the unadulterated flavour of the inimitable home produced meat. The flavours of spices and herbs have been added for their own sake and for no ulterior motive.

But now, with deep freezing reducing the full flavour of raw meat and fish, herbs and spices are enjoying a spontaneous revival.

Herbs and spices are being grown and dried now in England, Canada and the United States, from where they are being exported in quantity.

The History of the Herbalist

The art and superstitions of herbalists must be as old as time itself. Even in Genesis 1, 11 we are told, 'And God said, Let the earth bring forth grass, the herb yielding seed, and the fruit tree yielding fruit after his kind, whose seed is in itself, upon the earth: and it was so.' And verse 29, 'And God said, Behold, I have given you every herb bearing seed, which is upon the face of all the earth.'

Since then trees, herbs and flowers have all played a great part for good and evil in the history of mankind.

From the beginning, man had an affinity with living plants, for it was on them, together with meat from wild animals, that he depended largely for his food. And gradually, through trial and error, he must have learned which were poisonous, which were nourishing and good to eat, and which had healing or helpful properties.

The first and greatest true medical doctor of all time, known as 'The Father of Medicine', was the Greek, Hippocrates, in the 4th century B.C. He was certainly learned on the subject of herbs since he left a list of some four hundred 'simples' (herbs used medicinally).

Following him, Theophrastus of Athens (4th–3rd century B.C.), a pupil of Aristotle, was one of the most important contributors to ancient botanical science. He wrote the earliest work in existence on the subject – his ten volume 'History of Plants'. How much he learned from Aristotle nobody knows, because only a few fragments of Aristotle's work on botany remain.

In China, India and Egypt the early works on medicines and herbs from four or more centuries B.C. are known to have been of a high order. Before this era the knowledge of medicine undoubtedly possessed by the ancient Egyptians, Babylonians, Assyrians, Sumerians and others was very great, but it can only be judged through excavations, engravings and inscriptions on stone and clay.

The Greek physician, Pedacius Dioscorides, said to have been the private physician of Antony and Cleopatra, left, early in the 1st century A.D., what may be regarded as the earliest herbal in existence. His compilation of six hundred or so plants remained the source of herbal therapy for many centuries thereafter.

It was the monks who more than probably were the first to have special herb gardens at their monasteries for medical use, where they grew the herbs for treating illness and healing wounds. The Benedictine Order at Monte Cassino in the eighth century was possibly one of the first, followed by most of the large monasteries and convents, although even before that date physic gardens were known to have been cultivated in France, and in England under the Romans. The first public herb gardens, however, were founded in Padua in 1533.

Neither did the monks omit to learn how to use herbs for culinary matters. Nobody could fail to have heard of, if not actually enjoyed, the famous Chartreuse liqueur made by the Carthusian monks, amongst numerous other liqueurs distilled at various monasteries.

In England, Alfred the Great (849–899) was known to have used a 'Leech Book' which listed some five hundred healing herbs.

William Turner, between 1551 and 1568, was the first man to publish a herbal in English (before that time herbal books had been written in Latin, German and Italian) listing plants alphabetically, and for the first time also recording their origin.

But it was John Gerard, the English herbalist and surgeon, who in 1597 was the first to produce a really comprehensive and profound book on herbs and their properties. His great 'Herball' was fully illustrated and he gave details of each plant with its origin, history, use, methods of planting, and the best type of soil for each.

He, like other apothecaries of his time, had a garden where he grew and studied the plants. Gerard's garden was in Holborn, in the City of London, on the banks of the river Fleet. He was also apothecary to James I, during whose reign the Worshipful Company of Apothecaries founded their famous Physic Garden.

It should perhaps be mentioned that Gerard's name might not have become so famous had not another London apothecary, Thomas Johnson (who also had his own garden at Snow Hill), re-illustrated, re-edited, and re-issued Gerard's book in 1633, twenty-one years after his death. Nevertheless, it was Gerard who was the inspiration of every writer on herbs thereafter. And there have been many.

Nicholas Culpeper (1616–1654) was both an astrologer and a physician, and in the various books which he wrote on herbals he grouped plants by astrological influence. He also tried to surround with magic and mystery the old art of healing with 'simples'. This brought him into conflict with the medical practitioners of his time, and also the practice of herbal cures under disrepute.

The seventeenth century saw the height of the use of herbals for curative medicine, some famous physic gardens growing as many as sixteen hundred different plants.

But with the advance of scientific knowledge, medicine developed beyond the use of the natural properties of pure plants, which through the preceding centuries had been the only means whereby physicians had been able to help their patients. Synthetic substances were then evolved, which contained the active principles of the drugs previously found only in nature. And others were invented from entirely new substances.

Thus the use of pure herbs and plants began to decline, and plants started to be grown for the sake of the beauty of their flowers alone.

Herbs, however, are enjoying a big revival as more and more people are becoming interested in them, largely in the culinary field. This is probably because, as travel becomes more universal, the thrill of tasting the exciting flavours of the foods of different countries is being experienced with such pleasure, that the joy of reproducing them at home is greatly increasing sales of herbs and spices. And let us not forget that the fore-fathers of the British used dozens of herbs and spices in their dishes (although for a special reason!), and took many of these with them when they emigrated to the United States to found the basis of their cuisine, which now uses spices with lavish abandon.

In some cases, the revival (or perhaps the practice has never died out) of the use of herbs and plants in the medical field is being thought of again. After all, penicillin, that wonderful drug which opened up a whole new vista for curative antibiotics, was discovered and grown from natural plant-mould on melon.

And Queen Elizabeth II, when in November 1955 she visited the Royal London Homoeopathic Hospital (of which she is patron), was presented with a beautifully arranged bouquet of forty-two flowers, leaves and berries, all used today in homoeopathic medicine.

Legends, Fables and Witchcraft

The facts and fables of plant life in all its aspects are inextricably interwoven.

At some moment in his evolution, man must have realized, and begun to ponder upon, the strange phenomena of the trees, shrubs and plants which lose their leaves, and therefore seemingly their life in winter, yet come to life again in the spring; whilst others remain green all through the year.

These facts assuredly lead to the belief that there must be gods from whom life itself springs.

In the less enlightened centuries of the past, placating these gods for the well-being of life-giving crops was all important to superstitious man. Gradually seasonal festivals were inaugurated to propitiate the gods for their favours in the different seasons, particularly the all-important season of fertility in the spring.

Horrible human sacrifices were perpetrated to this end, since as plants were vital to the life of man, it was held that so must they be equally necessary to the gods. Thus different plants became associated with ritual ceremonies, for the worship of each of these celestial beings.

Flowers also had an important association with the ancient mysteries, meticulous care being taken over both the variety of the flower and the scent. Myrtle was associated with the goddess Venus for example, and roses with Isis. The Druids made play with verbena in their rituals, whilst jasmine flowers figured prominently in Buddhist ceremonies, besides the mystical lotus flower of India, symbolized in their religious carvings and paintings.

As time progressed and man became more civilized, the idea of a variety of ferocious gods continually needing appeasement was superseded by the concept of an all-powerful benign Being (albeit in different guises), who preferred kindness to cruelty.

But even to this day, incense, made from a mixture of herbs and spices, is used in religious services, and special flowers are still connected with the anniversaries of the Christian Church. The Trinity is symbolized by the pansy, the violet dedicated to Easter and the lily of the valley to Ascension Day.

Witches played a great part in the superstitions of the past, and are we not all guilty of some superstitious practices ourselves, even though we may not actually be aware of it?

Old-time witches relied heavily upon natural plant life for their armoury of magic and potions – for example, their well-known escapades of flying on a broomstick. The broomstick was certainly made from one of the witches' special trees, either elder or hawthorn. Their password to each other that they had 'slept like a log' meant that they had been out on one of their nefarious activities, because they would use a log (as we might have used a bolster in our youth!) to leave in their bed, topped with a nightcap, to deceive anyone into thinking that they were peacefully asleep. So our natural reply to a kind enquiry about our night's rest, 'I slept like a log thank you', is unwittingly a relic of witchcraft!

Some of the earliest associations with magic took the form of poisons and the antidotes to them. These were meted out by witches and sorcerers in every part of the world. In fact, it was the terrible goddess Gula, the Sumerian goddess of sorcery, about 4500 B.C., who was the earliest diety to be connected with such evil doings. In ancient Greek and Roman legends, Hecate was the sorceress who discovered poison and, with her daughters Medea and Circe, practised every kind of wickedness with their concoctions of poison made from plants.

The early Caesars seem to have taken to this practice pretty thoroughly. They poisoned anyone who got in their way or whom they disliked, or even just for the fun of it – often ordering their own physician to administer it!

In the East, the Chinese and Hindus were past masters at concocting and administering poisons, although theirs were more often made from animals rather than solely from plants. Aconite root, opium, mandrake, belladonna and hemlock were the plants most commonly used for a poison potion.

In the Renaissance period, poisoning was a common method of removing an enemy or an unwanted mistress or lover. In Europe, Italy led the field in the art of poisoning and sold the poisons and the recipes for them to other nations.

So great was the fear of being poisoned that, in the sixteenth and seventeenth centuries, rich households used to employ special wine and food tasters, who had to taste each goblet of wine or dish of food before their masters would touch it.

But probably a witch's most valuable single aid was a mandrake (*Mandragora officinarum*), undoubtedly the plant with the most evil reputation of any.

The Arabs call it the 'devil's testicles'. It was said to shriek when pulled from the ground, so had to be drawn out by a dog tethered to a tree hauling on ropes fixed to the plant, because by reputation it would kill any human who attempted to dig it up. It often grew like a man with long legs, so was unsurpassed for inclusion in love-potions, as an aphrodisiac and to facilitate pregnancy.

Mandrake was used in the East as a narcotic, and Pliny the Elder (1st century B.C.) also mentioned it as a sort of anaesthetic, to cause insensitivity in people undergoing operations. If too much was eaten or if it was eaten with pickles, it was said to send a man mad. Obviously it had every charm for a witch!

Witches, and later apothecaries, were also much in demand through the ages to produce aphrodisiacs and love-potions. At one time the Greeks and Romans used a mixture of pepper, myrrh, perfume and magic as an aphrodisiac, and drank the mixture out of scented earthenware goblets. Glands of pigs, horses, hyenas and other animals were another favourite mixture. Winged ants, Spanish fly and later ambergris were all favoured as promoters of amorous passions.

But the list of ingredients for love-potions was legion. Each period and each country had its popular combinations and each, of course, mixed with magical spells.

Herbs and spices were also used in countless medical forms, and for their antiseptic and disinfectant qualities. For example, because at one time London used to be an 'insanitary and foul-smelling place', the floor of the Guildhall is even today strewn with aromatic herbs before the Lord Mayor's election, also the Queen carries a herb posy for the Maundy Thursday distribution of money to the poor.

In Scandinavia and other European countries, many of the remote churches used to be built without windows, and the dead were buried under the floor to save the bodies from being dug up by wild animals. Imagine the agony of having to sit through a service with a decomposing body beneath your feet! To alleviate the suffering from the stench, each person used to take a bunch of strong-smelling flowers and herbs to sniff during the service.

Many plants and flowers, perfectly harmless outdoors, seem prone to bring disaster when they are brought indoors. The lovely may (hawthorn), which nobody can fail to enjoy in its profuse flowering beauty, has for centuries been an indoor flower of ill omen portending the death of one of the household. Since when? Possibly from the days when the Druids used to choose a perfect couple, a young man and a virgin, who were crowned King and Queen with may blossoms. For the following year they were fêted and made much of. At the end of the year, they were put to death as a sacrifice to appease the gods and ensure fertility. Little wonder that in the following centuries, after such a rite, may was connected with death.

When the Christian church became powerful, it tried to eradicate the evil practices of the Druids and ordered their sacred groves to be cut down and burned, often building a church upon the site. Heavy penalties were imposed upon anyone practising the revolting cult of Black Magic with its direct affiliation with the Devil, and its superstitious practices involving plants and flowers.

A herb with a turbulent history of love and passion is basil. It is said that Salomé, after her gruesome dance with its prize of the head of John the Baptist, hid his head in a pot of basil. It could have been that basil, with its pungent scent, grew wild around the palace of King Herod; although I saw none nor did I hear that story when I visited the ruins of the palace at Samaria a few years ago. However, it seems a popular herb in which to keep heads of murdered men! In Keats's poem 'Isabella, or the Pot of Basil', Isabella kept the head of her murdered lover in a pot of basil and watered it with her tears.

On the other hand, in Italy a sprig of basil worn by a young man when calling on his girl friend, showed that his intentions were serious. When worn it is also supposed to die instantly if the wearer be 'light of love' (I have heard that about any flower!). In the East, basil is a talisman against witchcraft.

The list of good, protective plants is headed by angelica. Even the down-to-earth, unsuperstitious Gerard admits that angelica is efficacious against witchcraft.

Legend has it that its virtues were revealed to a monk, and so it became known as the 'Holy Ghost plant'. At all events in the early herbals, angelica, and particularly its root, was described as having more medicinal uses than any other plant. The root was a remarkable remedy against poison, the plague, the bite of a mad dog, and it seemed to help every part of the system from heart to spleen.

The bay tree is another talisman against destruction. The old saying 'Neither witch nor devil, thunder nor lightening will hurt a man in the place where a bay tree is' means that it would be a wise precaution to plant a bay tree in our garden. And to prove the point, that great Roman statesman, the Emperor Tiberius, was said to have been so terrified of thunder, that when a storm raged he crawled under his bed and covered his head with bay leaves!

Of course, the bay tree must be something special, because mythology states that the nymph Daphne was turned into a bay tree to save her from the pursuit of the god Apollo; since when the bay tree has naturally been Apollo's favourite tree. Ovid tells the story with great beauty.

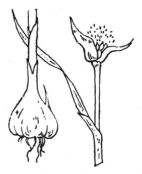

Garlic is another plant which appears to be not only good for health (see page 13) but also to have been a powerful antidote for poison. The Greek god, Hermes, is said to have taught the hero Odysseus to counteract the potions of Circe, daughter of sorceress Hecate, with garlic. Dioscorides, private physician to Antony and Cleopatra, in his compilation of plants praised garlic, amongst others, for its virtues.

Theophrastus and Aristotle mention that the men who went to cut some of the dangerous plants and gather some of the precious roots, so much prized in their day, used to rub themselves with oil or consume large quantities of garlic as a protection. And so the story repeats itself down to the present day. There must surely be something in the theory? What a pity it has THAT odour!

Herbs and How to Grow Them

Most herbs are easy to grow, but it is wise to buy seeds or plants from a reputable grower, to avoid the disappointment of inferior varieties being substituted.

Most herbs, with few exceptions, prefer a light rather poor soil and, when growing in a garden, do not like to be fertilized. But like all living things, they appreciate water.

With the exception of sorrel, they like lime, so dust the soil with lime when planting and give the earth around them a dusting of lime every year or two, for best results.

The best time to plant most seeds, or to divide the plants of the perennial varieties, is in the spring months, according to the weather.

Plan your herb garden as near to the kitchen door as possible. In wet weather, it is a bore to have to put on boots and other paraphernalia to go and pluck a few sprigs or leaves – they might not get used if weather or time were inauspicious for a trek.

Balm (Lemon Balm) *Melissa officinalis*. There are two or three types of balm, but the only one for culinary herb cultivation is the common or lemon balm.

This perennial plant is a native of southern Europe, but is now grown in nearly all temperate climates around the world.

Balm is very easy to grow, either from seed planted in late spring, or by dividing the roots in spring or autumn. It likes a modicum of shade, grows to two to two-and-a-half feet high and should be cut right down in the autumn.

Lemon balm is a delight in the garden for the aroma of its leaves, which are also a valuable ingredient for a pot-pourri. And whereas we appreciate the leaves, bees are inordinately fond of the nectar in the flowers. In fact, balm honey was once preferred to all others and bee hives were often rubbed with the leaves.

The crinkled bright green leaves are good for flower arrangements and, when infused, were also much used for balm tea as a heart stimulant.

It is a good plant for growing in a window box or pot. The leaves can be dried.

Basil (Sweet Basil) *Ocimum basilicum*. Basil came originally from India where it is sacred and features in religious rites and superstitions. But for many centuries it has grown wild in countries around the Mediterranean. In France, a pot of basil is often kept on tables of pavement restaurants – to keep flies away.

There are some forty types of basil, but the two given here are those most easily grown for culinary use.

Sweet basil is a half-hardy annual which likes sunshine. The seeds should not be sown outside in England until the danger of frost is over. They may be grown in a box in warmth and planted out in late spring.

Once it has established itself, it is best to nip out the tops to make the plant bush out, and also to delay its flowering for as long as possible. It grows to about three feet.

Basil is one of the most important herbs in cooking. It is used extensively in Italian, French and Greek cooking, where a tomato dish or sauce is seldom made without it.

It is particularly good for growing in window boxes and pots. The sprigs and leaves dry well.

Bush Basil *Ocimum minimum*. This is a miniature variety which grows only six to eight inches high. It has a less robust growth with much smaller leaves than sweet basil.

The flavour of the leaves is delightful, particularly mixed with other herbs, but they are not usually dried.

Bay Leaves *Laurus nobilis*. The bay tree, or sweet bay, is one of the laurel family and the only one whose leaves may be used in cooking.

A native of the Mediterranean area, the leaves used to be made into wreaths for the crowning of poets and heroes in ancient Greece and Rome – hence the honour 'Poet Laureate'.

The tree does not like hard frost, so it is wise to give it some protection: in the shade of other trees or away from chilling draughts.

It makes an attractive ornamental tree if grown in a tub as a standard, cutting off any laterals to encourage it to form a ball on top of a slender stem. Trees grown in this fashion are often seen on either side of the front door of a house, or the entrance to an hotel, restaurant or penthouse.

The leaves can be used fresh or dried.

Borage *Borago officinalis*. Borage is a native of the Mediterranean area and was originally cultivated by civilized Europeans for its medicinal rather than its culinary uses.

At one time, with other herbs, it was considered what we would call today a 'wonder drug'. It was also

11

considered an anti-depressant; perhaps the ancestor of our pep pills!

An annual, it is hardy and seeds itself easily. The plants grow to one-and-a-half to two feet and have clusters of lovely sky-blue flowers which make it ideal for growing in a garden, kitchen or herb garden, and for floral arrangements.

Bees adore the honey in the flowers.

Borage has a light cucumber flavour and the leaves and flowers are almost an essential garnishing ingredient of summer cups – Pimm's No. 1, claret cups, and so on.

The leaves are not good dried, but the flowers can be crystallized.

Burnet *Sanguisorba minor*. Burnet came originally from Asia and Europe, and the leaves have a flavour resembling cucumber.

It is a perennial which grows only one to one-and-a-half feet high, but spreads well. The leaves are large, roundish, serrated and low spreading and are also attractive for floral arrangements.

It is one of the few herbs which prefer a heavier soil.

The leaves are not good dried, but when fresh they make a compatible mixture with tarragon and rosemary, and the Italians are very fond of burnet mixed with their salads.

Chervil *Anthriscus cerefolium*. Chervil is a native of eastern and southern Europe and was one of the principal herbs brought to England by the Romans.

The leaves and seeds of chervil were much used medicinally in the past. Pliny said that hiccoughs could be stopped by drinking vinegar containing chervil seeds. It was used particularly in Lenten dishes for its blood-cleansing properties.

It is a hardy biennial and, if planted in late summer, will be ready for picking as one of the first herbs in the spring. Then sown again in early spring, it will give a continuous cycle through the summer and autumn. It also sows itself very easily if the seeds are allowed to dry on the plant.

Chervil grows to one to one-and-a-half feet, and in appearance is akin to the flat variety of parsley, with fern-like feathery leaves. In fact, in France it is often used in place of parsley, which by some is considered overdone as a garnish.

The leaves have a delicate anise flavour and it is one of the essential herbs for the French 'fines herbes' mixture. Delicious soups and sauces can also be made with chervil, so it should be planted in greater quantity than a herb used only for occasional flavouring.

It is much easier to grow than parsley. The seeds germinate quickly, although it likes semi-shade in the summer and sun in the winter. Like parsley, the leaves should be picked from the outside, so allowing it to keep growing from the centre.

It is an ideal plant for growing in window boxes and pots. The leaves dry well and retain their colour.

Chives *Allium schoenoprasum*. There are various types of chives, but the best known for growing as a herb is the one described here.

Chives were known in China as long ago as 3000 B.C., but apparently did not arrive in Europe until the 16th century. Since then, however, they have conquered the heart of every chef and every cook who appreciates the flavour of onion.

They are a hardy perennial, growing from tiny bulbs which are matted together by fibrous roots. It is best to divide them in the autumn, preserving the outside bulbs of each clump. They are one of the few herbs which like a fairly rich soil.

The flowers are a pretty mauve colour, growing like little pincushions on the end of each stem. They make an attractive display in a vase, especially when mixed with some grey-green foliage or with other flowers. And it is amusing to note how few people ever recognize the flowers!

If the flowers are not to be used, or if there are sufficient plants for both decorative and culinary use, cut down some to ground level as soon as the flowers appear. The leaves will start to grow again in a week and will remain green and tender instead of drying off, as they are apt to do while the plant flowers.

Chives have a definite onion flavour, but much milder, and those who dislike onion or find it disturbs their digestion, can often eat and enjoy the hollow grass-like leaves, cut or chopped into small lengths. They are matchless used raw in salads of every kind, as a garnish for soups, hors d'oeuvre and mixed with creamed cheese. In fact, of all the herbs, chives and parsley are indispensable in every kitchen.

They grow nine to twelve inches high and make a good border plant. They are also ideal for window boxes and pots.

The leaves can be dried, but I do not recommend it.

Dill *Anethum graveolens*. Dill is a native of the Mediterranean and Black Sea areas, and much has been written about it in history.

It was well known in Pliny's time and, in England, William the Conqueror is said to have introduced it to his cook with highly successful results. In America, there is a charming saying that the seeds of dill and fennel were called 'Meetin' seed' because they were given to the children to ward off the pangs of hunger during the lengthy sermons of earlier days!

The Scandinavian countries use it not only for flavouring, but even more frequently than parsley for decoration. I have met its pretty thread-like feathery-leaved sprays as decoration from Kirkness in the north of Norway, to south Zealand in Denmark. The whole of central Europe is also dedicated to the traditional flavour of dill.

The leaves – or as they are called when dried, dill weed – have the faintest flavour of caraway, but seem to combine a slight sweetness with an aromatic sharpness. The seeds have a more pungent flavour.

Dill is known to be good for the digestion and dill water for babies is a byword. It is also famous the world over for pickling. Dill pickle, with cucumber, stands on its own for many people and countries.

It is an annual which grows to a height of two-and-a-half to three feet. The seeds should be planted in early spring or summer where they are to remain, without fear of frost, as they dislike being moved. Thin out later, leaving a foot between each plant. It likes to be well drained and well watered.

Dill should not be planted near fennel for two reasons. First, cross-pollination takes place, so the following year the plants will be neither true dill nor fennel. Secondly, when you collect the seeds from the drying-off plants, they are so similar that it is difficult to tell them apart.

The seeds can be gathered and dried easily. The leaves can also be dried.

Fennel *Foeniculum vulgare*. Fennel is one of the oldest herbs known and might be rated as one of the classics.

It is a native of the Mediterranean countries and was taken to many other lands by the conquering Romans. Probably brought by the Romans, it now grows wild in England along country roadsides.

There are many old and odd legends about fennel, apart from its reputation as a cure of eye ailments, for reducing weight, helping the digestion and acting as an important ingredient for cosmetics.

There are two main varieties, the perennial *Foeniculum vulgare* and the annual *Foeniculum vulgare dulce*, known as Florence fennel or Finocchio.

The perennial is a graceful sturdy plant, easy to grow and growing to four to six feet. The feathery leaves and the seeds are most used commercially.

The annual, Florence fennel, is less robust and grows to about half the height of the perennial. It likes a sunny position with plenty of moisture and when the base begins to swell, the soil should be cultivated and fed. These solid, white, bulbous looking lower stems do not usually grow as big in England as in France or Italy, where they are very popular as a vegetable; both raw in salads and hors d'oeuvre, and cooked cut in slices. But they are gaining in popularity in the British Isles since larger greengrocers are selling them more regularly.

For centuries, the leaves have been closely associated with fish, particularly the more oily kinds; presumably to alleviate any digestive difficulties which might be suffered from the richness of the oil.

Both the stem and leaves have a distinct anise flavour which also enhances many sauces and meat dishes as well as fish. In fact, fennel and dill are interchangeable.

Fronds of fennel, especially the perennial variety, are much appreciated for flower arrangements.

It can be grown in a pot or window box, if cut down to eight to ten inches.

Both the leaves and the seeds dry well.

Garlic *Allium sativum*. Garlic is a sister or brother to the onion, shallot, leek and chive, but in flavour is stronger, far more pungent and utterly irreplaceable for putting zest into the dullest dish.

It is a bulb which is made up of many smaller bulbs of varying sizes called 'cloves'. Recipes calling for 'a clove of garlic' mean one of these and *not* the whole bulb.

Plant them as you would onions, in a rich friable soil, pressing the cloves in to a depth of about two inches and about six inches apart. When the tops are dry, lift them and dry thoroughly, removing the roots. Store, wrapped in foil, in a dry place.

Garlic is normally used in Britain in such small quantities and can always be bought from a greengrocer, that it seems to me unnecessary to use space growing it in a small garden. On the Continent, where it is used almost as freely as we use salt and pepper, and in Russia where they serve masses of whole cloves in a sauce with chicken, it is a MUST of course.

Garlic is one of the most valuable of medicinal herbs and many people in Europe swallow, and give their children, a whole clove every day. Their adage is more 'A garlic a day keeps the doctor away' than our apple!

There are many ideas on how to remove the odour of garlic from the breath: swallow a whole *uncut* clove before *one* mouthful of food containing garlic is eaten; chew a coffee bean or sprig of parsley after eating. All help, I have found, but true garlic lovers know that nothing but time will completely eradicate that unmistakable odour!

Horseradish *Armoracia rusticana*. The perennial horseradish is perhaps not strictly a herb. However, as it is used not as a vegetable but as a seasoning in many dishes, apart from the traditional horseradish sauce with beef, it may be permissible to include it here.

The roots are the part used in cooking, fresh or dried. They look much like a parsnip and like all deep growing roots they like a friable, well drained soil, so that they can push down easily.

Perennial is the correct word. If horseradish likes your soil, it will ramp and grow roughshod over anything which grows in its way, so be careful to watch it.

The flavour is very strong, like mustard, and if eaten in too large a mouthful it will cause great discomfort up the nose and out of the eyes! But a little, especially in a sauce, can make the difference between something prosaic and something exciting.

Horseradish is always grated, minced or ground, fresh or dried. But as ever, there is no comparison between the fresh and the dried root.

Hyssop *Hyssopus officinalis*. The name 'hyssop' is glamorized by the many references to it in the Bible, although there seems confusion as to whether the hyssop we grow today is the same as that used in biblical times.

It was also much used by monks in Europe and is one of the numerous herbs used by them in the famous Chartreuse liqueur.

It is a perennial plant, growing to one-and-a half to two feet and thrives best in partial shade.

There are several varieties, but the hardiest and prettiest is the one which has clusters of blue flowers. Bees and flower arrangers both appreciate its various attractions.

In Europe, the oil is extracted from the plant for use in toilet preparations and the leaves are used in cooking. They have a slightly minty flavour which is said to aid the digestion of fat.

Lovage *Levisticum officinale*. Lovage is a hardy perennial which grows to a height of about four feet. The leaves and the flavour are very reminiscent of celery. In fact, if there is space, it is a valuable component of a herb or kitchen garden, because it can be used in place of celery as a vegetable as well as a flavouring.

The great herbalist, John Gerard, in his 'Herball' wrote of it as another of the wonder drugs with properties also conducive, or at least helpful, to love! It is said to be a deodorant with a cleansing effect upon the whole system. In former times perhaps this herb took the place of some of our well known BO advertisements of today!

The stems can be candied like angelica or used fresh as a vegetable. The leaves and seeds can be used fresh for flavouring (but use more sparingly than celery as it has a harsher, stronger flavour), and the seeds can be dried.

Marjoram (Sweet or Knotted) *Organum marjorana*. There are three main kinds of marjoram which are widely used and grown. The sweet or knotted (so called because the flower heads are produced in pairs as greenish clusters when they first appear, looking like knots) is the most useful in cooking and therefore the most useful for cultivation.

Marjoram is a native of the Mediterranean area where it has been known for centuries. Venus, goddess of love, is accredited as having grown it on Mount Olympus. The Indian gods, Siva and Vishnu, are also said to hold it as sacred. And Shakespeare, in 'All's Well that Ends Well', has the Clown saying to old Lord Lafeu: 'Indeed, sir, she was the sweet marjoram of the salad, or, rather the herb of grace.'

In warmer climates it grows as a perennial, but it cannot withstand frost and therefore in colder climates it is treated as an annual. It can be planted in very early spring under glass and then transplanted to the garden in late spring, or planted outdoors in mid-spring.

It grows into a bushy plant twelve to eighteen inches high and has either white, pale pink, or lilac flowers.

The fresh leaves have an aromatic combination of flavours which is somewhat lost in character when they are dried. Nevertheless, marjoram is one of the most widely used of herbs both by private cooks and food producers.

Pot Marjoram *Origanum onites*. Pot marjoram is a perennial and much more robust than sweet marjoram, although it is apt to straggle. According to Pliny, it was used a lot medicinally.

It grows to about two feet and has flat-topped clusters of pinkish-mauve flowers. The roots should be divided in the spring.

The flavour of the leaves in cooking is stronger tasting than that of sweet marjoram, so it should be used with discretion.

Both varieties grow well in window boxes and pots. The leaves should be dried for constant use.

Wild Marjoram *Origanum vulgaris*. See Oregano page 15.

Mint (Spearmint) *Mentha spicata*. There are over twenty varieties of mint and many more crossbreeds, but only three or four are normally cultivated.

Mint was mentioned in the New Testament, but nobody seems to know from where it actually came, since it has never been found in an original wild state.

It was used by the Greeks, Indians, Chinese and Europeans, not only in cooking but also medicinally for combating and curing all sorts of diseases.

Now it is grown in profusion in Great Britain and the United States of America. Today, new potatoes boiled without a sprig of mint added to the water, would constitute almost an insult to the potatoes! Many people, too, would scorn roast lamb without mint sauce.

The most usual type of mint to be grown commercially for sale fresh in greengrocers, and for drying, is the spicata, which grows to a height of two to two-and-a-half feet.

It likes a slightly richer soil than most other herbs and ramps like mad, the roots running underground to send up numerous shoots. The best way to contain a plant, to stop it spreading too far, is to plant it in a large pot and sink it into the ground.

Mint propagation is by root division. The plants should be cut back in autumn and when the fresh shoots appear in the spring, they should be cut from the tough old roots and replanted. This helps to stop 'rust', to which spearmint is rather prone.

It can be grown in a window box, but should be planted in a pot and sunk into the box, so that the roots cannot suffocate any other herb. Or grow it in a pot. All mint leaves can be dried.

Round Leaved Mint *Mentha rotundifolia.* This is usually sold as 'apple mint' but the name is incorrect. It is, as its name implies, a round type of mint whose leaves are a bit hairy. It grows to the same height as spearmint and in every way is comparable, except that the flavour of the leaves is stronger and to my mind superior. I cannot understand why it is not more widely favoured.

Use it in place of spearmint, in exactly the same ways.

Apple Mint *Mentha alopecuroides.* This is the true apple mint, which is a most attractive looking plant with its variegated green leaves bordered by cream and cream coloured flowers.

It grows only to about eighteen inches and is most useful for flower decorations.

The leaves have a distinct aroma and taste of apple with overtones of mint. It is an excellent type with which to make mint sauce; some people think it is the best type of all the mints for this particular sauce.

Peppermint *Mentha piperita.* Peppermint is used primarily by the pharmaceutical and confectionery trades, the oil being distilled from the plants. This oil is used to disguise many an unpleasant taste in medicines. Then, after Ray, the great botanist, had recognised it as a distinct species, it was officially included in the London Pharmacopoeia in 1721. It is also the source of the many peppermint flavoured sweets which we enjoy.

The plant grows to the same height or a little taller than spearmint, with a reddish tinge on the stems and has flowers of a rosy lavender colour. It is cultivated in exactly the same way as other mints.

Peppermint tea is considered the best of the mint teas and is good either hot or cold. But it should not be made too strong.

Onion, Welsh or Ever Ready. This is not strictly a herb, but I use the evergreen leaves which look like a rather coarser chive, during the winter, in place of chives, although they are not a good substitute for flavour. Miraculously, they seem to survive the hardest weather.

The onions grow together in clumps, exactly like shallots, but unlike them do not have to be taken up and dried each year. The well-named ever ready onion is a valuable alternative to an ordinary onion in an emergency.

These onions can be grown in window boxes or pots, but the green cannot be dried.

Oregano *Origanum vulgare.* Oregano is the wild marjoram (see page 14). It is a native of the Mediterranean area and also now grows wild in chalky areas in England. Doubtless it was one of the Romans' favourite herbs which they took with them wherever they went.

This perennial grows to a height of one-and-a-half to two feet, with lavender coloured flowers in clusters. It is easy to cultivate.

Oregano has a somewhat different, more biting taste than marjoram, especially when dried. I regard it as indispensable in the kitchen, together with parsley and chives. Certainly one could not think of making that favourite Spaghetti Bolognese or Pizza without it.

It can be grown well in a window box or pot. The leaves are excellent dried.

Parsley *Petroselinum crispum.* There are several kinds of parsley of which the crinkled, curly-leafed type is the best known and most widely used. Dwarf Perfection is a new strain of this type which is hardy and compact.

Then there is the Italian or flat-leafed type (*Petroselinum crispum neopolitanum*), superior in flavour but not nearly so pretty for decoration.

The turnip-rooted, or Hamburg parsley, which is really more of a vegetable than a herb, has a large tap root like a carrot which can be lifted and stored like other root vegetables. The root is definitely parsley flavoured and can also be grated or sliced finely for salads.

Parsley is one of the oldest of all the herbs and is known to have been in cultivation for at least 2000 years. It is a native of the Mediterranean area and both the Greeks and Romans used it for all sorts of things other than culinary decoration.

The Greek gods were said to have fed it to their horses to make them swift of foot and full of spirit. The Romans wore it as a necklace to ward off intoxication, and down the ages it has been used as a family medicine. In England, it has been used as a tea for the help of rheumatism and indigestion and as a diuretic tonic.

The ancients, of course, had never heard of

vitamins, but they were right in treating parsley as a medicine and as a buck-you-up stimulant, for it is rich in vitamins A and C, iron, and valuable organic salts.

Strictly, parsley is a biennial, but it is usually treated as an annual because it will not stand a hard frost unless it is protected.

It is slow in germinating and often does not come up at all. There is an old Shropshire saying which personifies this: 'Parsley must be sown six times, for the Devil takes all but the last!' And another old country saying is that if a man cannot grow parsley, the woman wears the trousers! Yet another strongly held belief is that parsley must always be sown on a waxing and not a waning moon.

Try at least to get the better of the Devil by sowing your parsley seed this way: sow first in early spring and then four months later. It must be left where it is sown for it hates being moved, so as soon as the seed germinates be ruthless in thinning out.

Make a narrow shallow trench with a trowel, fill it with a suitable mixture; in England two-thirds John Innes seed compost and one-third silver sand. Sow the seed and cover by a quarter inch. Keep moist.

Cut back the early plants in the summer months, and the later sowing before the plants flower, and they will bush out again. Always pick parsley from the outside so as to allow the young leaves to grow in the centre.

There is more concentrated flavour in the stalks of parsley than in the leaves themselves, so use the stalks for flavouring stews and soups.

It is the most important herb for garnishing and grows well for a little time in a window box or pot.

Parsley does not dry really successfully, although now it is sold thus commercially. It is rarely that it cannot be either grown or bought in a shop, so it is hardly worth the effort of drying it.

There are several popular ways of keeping it after picking.
1. Keep the stems in a glass of water.
2. Wash, dry lightly, keep in a plastic box or bag in a refrigerator.
3. Wash and fold in a cloth. The cloth absorbs the moisture.
4. Freezing (see page 22).

Pennyroyal *Mentha pulegium*. Pennyroyal is another member of the mint family which is thought to have come originally from Europe and parts of Asia. It grows wild now in England.

It is the smallest member of the mint family, growing only to five or six inches, with circlets of pretty mauve flowers. It is good as an edging plant or between paving stones.

It has a more pungent flavour than other mints and tastes of peppermint.

Pennyroyal was formerly used as a deterrent to fleas in rooms, in straw mattresses and in the straw beds of dogs and other animals. It appears to have been effective from all accounts.

It can be grown in window boxes or pots, but the space would be better used for other herbs more often used in cooking. Pennyroyal can also be dried.

Rosemary *Rosmarinus officinalis*. Rosemary is a native of the Mediterranean areas, particularly in Spain and Italy, where the hillsides are covered with these fragrant little bushes, which smell heavenly in the heat after a shower of rain.

The legend of how rosemary got its name, comes from a heavenly source. It is said that when the Holy Family was fleeing to Egypt, the Virgin Mary hung her blue robe over a white flowering rosemary bush. In the morning the flowers had turned as blue as her gown, and thereafter the bush was known as the 'Rose of Mary'.

Rosemary is also known for remembrance. The unfortunate Ophelia in Shakespeare's 'Hamlet', driven mad by the death of her Father and Hamlet's rejection, cries, 'There's rosemary, that's for remembrance; pray, love, remember: and there is pansies, that's for thoughts'. Then again she says, 'There's fennel for you, and columbines; there's rue for you; and here's some for me; we may call it herb of grace o' Sundays. O! you must wear your rue with a difference.' Shakespeare with his knowledge of wild herbs gained from his youthful wanderings around the countryside, used them often to give effect to his descriptions of sentiment and atmosphere.

Because of its reputation for remembrance, rosemary is often included in a wreath for a funeral, and is still quite commonly used in France for such an occasion. In Australia, they frequently wear a sprig for remembrance on Anzac Day.

It is also said that rosemary will not grow in the garden of anyone who is evil or unlucky. But if given to one's beloved, it ensures faithfulness!

In any case, it is a perennial bush which grows to four or four-and-a-half feet with attractive pointed evergreen leaves, green on top and grey beneath, and makes a splendid background to any herb or kitchen garden. Bees adore it, so, leaving superstition aside, it is well worth growing for its beauty and lovely flavour in cooking.

Rosemary can be propagated by striking cuttings, with a 'heel' if possible, in late summer or autumn as the best time, but otherwise at any time in the spring. It is not too hardy and so likes a sunny sheltered spot. A really hard frost may kill it unless it is protected. Do not cut back until it is established, and then only for use or to keep in shape.

The flavour of rosemary gives a delicious fragrance to many dishes, especially lamb, veal and chicken.

Try it mixed with other herbs, whenever you want a savoury dish to be subtly alluring.

The leaves are prickly and pin-like and do not soften much in cooking, so unless they are being used as a flavouring only, it is best to cut them up finely. They can be quite painful if they get stuck into the gum, and the best way of ensuring that this does not happen is to cut them into small pieces. Do this by holding in a bunch as many leaves as you can and snipping them with a pair of scissors into a bowl.

Rosemary can be grown in a tub or pot, but must be pruned carefully to keep the bush compact. The leaves dry well.

Rue *Ruta graveolens.* Rue was known to the ancient Greeks and Romans as a seasoning, but more especially as a medicine. In Pliny's time, for example, it was used apparently for eighty-four ailments and was much valued for its magical properties!

It used to be known as the 'Herb of Grace' and was a symbol of repentance. Shakespeare used it as such in 'Hamlet' and mentions it upon several other occasions.

It is also known as 'stinking rue' from its bitter taste and a smell which many people dislike intensely, although for others it has a peculiar charm.

The perennial shrub came from southern Europe and grows wild along the roadsides in Italy, but it is not so much used now. However, in Elizabethan times they used it as a hedge around their small formal gardens, for it can stand being well clipped and has attractive blue-green lacy leaves. The yellow flowers are also pretty and continue all through the summer. It is an excellent plant for flower arrangements.

Rue grows to two feet high and can be planted by seed in a shallow drill or be propagated by taking cuttings – both in the spring. Also in the spring, the established plants should be cut back to eight to twelve inches. The leaves can be dried.

Sage *Salvia officinalis.* There are several varieties of sage but the broad leafed garden type is the best for the kitchen.

Sage came originally from the Mediterranean area and has been cultivated since the earliest days of recorded history. Theophrastus, the great Greek peripatetic philosopher, pupil of Aristotle, in the 3rd century B.C. wrote a lot about sage in his books on plants. Then Dioscorides, in the 1st century A.D., the first man to establish medical botany as an applied science, giving details of about six hundred medical plants, wrote at length on the properties of sage.

The name *salvia* is itself derived from the Latin word *salvere* – to save or heal. There is an old Arab proverb which has become a well accepted saying in many countries around the world, 'How can a man die if he has sage in his garden?' Old country folk used to include it in their daily diet, as proved by numerous ancient recipes for sage tea, wine, cheese and even tobacco!

Of course, the conquering Romans took it with them to every country in which they settled.

Sage is a perennial bush which grows normally to about two feet, but higher if it can be planted in a sunny, well-drained and sheltered position. It is best to replace the bushes every three or four years because after that time they are apt to become leggy and woody.

It is easy to propagate by cuttings struck in late spring. And the flower stalks should be cut off after flowering to encourage the bush to grow in a sturdy compact form.

Sage can be grown in window boxes if carefully pruned, but is better grown in pots.

The leaves can be dried with ease and success, but if care is not taken to do this at the right time and in the right way, the flavour is apt to seem musty. According to old writings, sage is best and at its most beneficial in the spring before it begins to flower, therefore should be picked for drying at this time.

Savory, Summer *Satureia hortensis.* There are two savories – summer and winter. The summer savory is an annual, growing to about twelve inches, whilst the winter savory is a perennial growing to about the same height or an inch or two taller.

Both are natives of the Mediterranean area where they are used extensively in cooking, particularly with beans of all kinds. In fact, in that section of the world, beans are boiled with savory almost as much as the English boil mint with new potatoes.

The flavour of summer savory is lighter, and one could describe it almost as more feminine than that of the harder more pungent, masculine winter savory. However, both are strong, with a peppery tang which can drown rather than draw out the flavour of a dish, so they should be used with care. It is a good herb also for those on a salt-free diet, as it can alleviate the flat taste of unseasoned food.

Sow seeds of summer savory in shallow, well drained soil in the spring.

It can be grown in pots indoors, to enjoy its fresh leaves throughout the winter.

This is the savory most used commercially for drying.

Savory, Winter *Satureia montana.* A hardy perennial plant which nevertheless should be divided every third year, using the outside shoots and discarding the tough centre.

This is one of the herbs which I pick fresh from the garden during the whole twelve months, whenever I want to use a mixture of herbs for any lightly cooked dish. The incomparable flavour of fresh herbs once enjoyed makes it imperative to grow *some* fresh herbs whenever possible.

Sorrel (French) *Rumex scutatus* **(Garden)** *Rumex acetosa*. There are three distinct varieties of sorrel. Two are cultivated and the third is the wild wood sorrel (*Oxalis acetosella*).

Sorrel is one of the few herbs which prefers a richer moist soil and can be grown in the shade. Both are hardy perennials, the garden variety being a larger plant growing to over two feet. Both should be dug up in early spring every four or five years and divided.

Perhaps the French variety is the better for all culinary purposes, as the leaves have more flavour than the larger garden one. It should be planted at least a foot apart. The leaves should be picked hard, or they dry off.

Sorrel has a slightly bitter flavour and is excellent when mixed with spinach, lettuce or cabbage. The French use it as a vegetable mixed with any of the above, in the same way as the English use spinach. Or as in their famous sorrel soup. Sorrel leaves make a very pleasant addition to lettuce salads or chopped into egg and fish dishes.

The leaves can be dried but I wouldn't recommend this.

Southernwood (Old Man. Lad's Love) *Artemisia abrotanum*. Southernwood is another of the old-fashioned herbs, grown now more for its sweet scent than for its use in cooking, as it has a bitter taste.

It is a hardy perennial growing in height to three or four feet, but it can be clipped to make a neat hedge or a rounded bush. For a hedge, the bushes should be planted twelve inches apart.

Cuttings, struck in autumn or early spring, root easily and thrive in any soil. It is not an evergreen as the leaves, somewhat resembling rosemary, fall in the winter.

This herb derives its delightful name of 'Old Man' from a reputation it once had of encouraging hair to grow on balding pates, and on the downy chins of young men! 'Lad's Love' came from the old habit of a young lover including a sprig in a bouquet for his lass.

Sweet Cicely (Great Chervil. Cow Chervil. Sweet Fern) *Myrrhis odorata*. Sweet cicely is a plant which goes far back in European and Middle Eastern history, even to biblical times. Now it grows wild also in England, where it is used more in the north than in the south.

It is a perennial growing to a height of two feet or over and has deeply divided leaves, which makes it another plant good for flower decorations. It is also one of the longest growing plants in the garden apart from the evergreens.

Sweet cicely has a sweetish flavour faintly reminiscent of anise, but this almost completely disappears during cooking, leaving only the sweetness. For this reason, it is a herb which can be used to reduce the tartness in fruits (see page 31). It is also one of the herbs used by the Carthusian monks in the making of the liqueur Chartreuse. Therefore it can well be used to flavour beverages of all kinds.

The leaves and the crushed seeds can both be used fairly lavishly for flavouring. Sweet cicely has been known down the ages as an excellent synergic when blended with other herbs. In fact, it is the one herb which seems to bring out the flavour of every other herb with which it is mixed. The seeds can be dried.

Tarragon *Artemisia dracunculus*. This is the aristocrat of herbs, said to be a native of southern Russia. It is one of the latest herbs in culinary usage and has been adopted primarily by the French for their haute cuisine. In fact, the French variety, as above, is infinitely superior to the Russian variety (*Artemisia dracunculoides*).

Tarragon is a perennial plant, growing to two to three feet. But it can be killed by hard frost, so it is best to give it some protection in really hard weather.

It is temperamental as to its choice of site and if it does not get the soil it likes, it simply refuses to grow. I tried five times to grow tarragon. The first four times the soil was too rich or too moist, the fifth time I dug good holes two feet apart, filled them with poor sandy soil and my tarragon grew and grew!

It does not grow from seed, so it must be bought as plants in the spring or by cadging a piece of root from a friend, or by taking cuttings in the late spring.

Tarragon vinegar is perhaps the way in which this herb is best known, but until the French way of using it is tried in Poulet or Rognons à l'Estragon, the superb flavour cannot be sufficiently appreciated. It is also an essential ingredient of many of their sauces such as Sauce Béarnaise or Tartare, and in innumerable other dishes, cooked and uncooked.

It is an excellent herb for growing in a window box or in a pot indoors, for use right through the winter.

The leaves dry well.

Thyme *Thymus vulgaris*. There are at least fifty varieties of thyme, all attractive in growth, aromatic in perfume and beautiful in flower.

It is a native of the stony places along the coasts of the Mediterranean countries, but has been cultivated for centuries in most civilized countries.

The name comes from two Greek words: *thymon* – to sacrifice – it was used as an incense to perfume the ancient temples, which I suspect needed perfuming after some of their sacrifices! Or as named by the Greek philosopher, Theophrastus, from the word *thuo*, to perfume. In either case, its function then was more as a relief to the spirit than a pleasure to the stomach.

The Romans believed that pillows stuffed with sweet scented thyme would aid sleep and banish melancholy. And through the succeeding centuries, the oil extracted from thyme has been used in perfumes and toilet articles and as a moth preventative.

All thymes are low growing, creeping, perennial plants but some are more miniature than others. The original wild *Thymus serpyllum* is one of the smallest varieties which forms a dense mat. It is called the 'Mother of Thyme' and is reputed to be Shakespeare's 'wild thyme' with magic associations. This is the best variety to plant between paving stones, beside a garden seat or to use as a thyme lawn. It has bright pink flowers in the summer and a gorgeously sweet scent which is especially strong when crushed.

Then there is a caraway thyme (*Thymus herba-barona*) which has an unmistakable scent and flavour of caraway overlaying the typical thyme flavour. In the old days, this used to be rubbed into a Baron of Beef to preserve it and to disguise a high flavour!

But the two most usual varieties for cultivation in a herb garden, for use in cooking, are the common garden thyme and lemon thyme (*Thymus citriodorus*) which has a strong scent of lemon and is not as pungent in flavour as the common variety.

These two grow twelve to eighteen inches high and are propagated by division of old roots or by cuttings taken any time during the early summer months; side shoots can be layered in the early spring months. The common variety can be grown from seed and planted in the spring, but lemon thyme will not grow from seed.

The bushes should be divided every two years or so because they are prone to become leggy and die back in patches. Cut back the bushes after flowering for compact growth, or before they flower if they are required only for cooking.

Bees love these flowers and thyme honey is a much sought after variety.

Thyme is one of the components of a bouquet garni, it should be one of the most common herbs, after parsley, to be found in any kitchen.

It is an excellent herb for growing in a window box or pot and one of the easiest and most rewarding for drying.

Growing Herbs in Pots, Window Boxes and Kitchen Gardens

The thought of herb growing might be a trifle daunting to some, but once tried it is apt to become an almost compulsive hobby.

There is something very satisfying in growing plants which have so many features. Herbs are not only for show like most plants. They may not look as dramatic as a Jersey Lily, but who can resist the heavenly blue of the borage flower or a pinky-mauve carpet of thyme? Add the soul-soothing pleasure of their scent upon a balmy evening (or when the wind blows their perfume into a room or kitchen), to the exquisite satisfaction from their subtle intrusion in any dish, to lift it right out of its normal class, and the fascination of growing herbs can perhaps be comprehended.

Many herbs can occupy a small place. Or a small space can happily be occupied by herbs. Let us start from the beginning.

If a bed-sitter or flat-dweller hankers after the joy of fresh herbs, the answer may be to have two or three pots by a window or on a sill or a window box easily tended from a window, or pots on a roof garden can look very attractive.

Which herbs to grow in them? This must depend upon the taste of each individual. Do you crave the light onion flavour of chives or would you prefer an all round lifter such as basil or marjoram? Are you an avid 'mint-saucer' with lamb or would you like fennel with your fish and chicken?

I can only suggest my own favourites in the list of most suitable herbs for pots and window boxes. From these, each person must select for their own requirements and space.

1. *Parsley*. As this herb is the one most usually found in greengrocers, it may not be so necessary to grow it, as parsley is also difficult to grow. But it is the most necessary of all for garnishing as well as for flavour.
2. *Chives*. They can only be bought at certain times of the year in shops, but can be grown to cut most of the way through the year in a pot, or until frost touches them in a window box.
3. *Thyme*.

4. *Marjoram or Oregano* – depending upon your taste in food. Plant oregano in a separate pot.
5. *Winter savory*. Plant in a separate pot.
6. *Tarragon.*
7. *Mint*. Plant in a separate pot.
8. *Fennel.*
9. *Chervil.*
10. *Sage.*
11. *Welsh onion.*

NOTE: In some States in Australia, fennel, penny-royal and sorrel are listed as noxious weeds and permission must be obtained to plant them.

Suggestions for Pots and Window Boxes. Keep the pots as near to the light and sunshine as convenient, putting them out into the rain periodically.

The number of herbs in each window box must, of course, depend upon the size of the box and its location, but always allow plenty of room for the roots to spread. There are a few herbs whose roots are so rampant that they will grow all over the others in a box and smother them. In these cases, plant each in a pot and then place into the window box.

Window boxes, so named, need not necessarily sit upon a window ledge or a balcony. They can also adorn a roof garden, however small, and can be hung on a garage, garden or house wall to brighten and lend interest to an otherwise dull expanse.

The boxes themselves can be made of wood, a composite material or concrete. Or pots can be placed in graceful wrought-iron containers standing upon legs, to form a feature in any room.

Pots can be made of the ordinary terra-cotta clay, or glazed and decorated pottery for a feature position. Square pots, made in concrete, can be very effective placed outside a kitchen door, on a roof garden or along the edge of any small terrace.

There is also another type of pot which can be both decorative and useful for herb growing. These are called 'strawberry pots' and have a number of pockets all around them. They are ideal for a balcony, roof garden or just outside a kitchen door. To arrange them, plant the most decorative one, or the herb you wish to use most, at the top.

In England, there are now firms selling composition window boxes complete with herb plants. Some of these window boxes include chives, pot marjoram, thyme, sage and tarragon.

Concrete containers have the advantage of lasting longer than their former better known wooden counterparts, especially in the open, and need no upkeep in painting or varnishing. They are also reasonably simple to make at home.

Hints for Planting. Cover the hole in the container with some broken bits of crockery, but not so tightly that the water cannot seep through. Then fill with soil.

The best soils to use are those proprietary brands which are especially blended for this type of plant. John Innes Compost No. 3, Levington Compost and EFF Compost are three of the most suitable in England.

Watering is important. Once a day is sufficient, with only enough to allow the water to seep through to the bottom. The plants should never stand in water.

Plant the herbs about two to three inches deep and press the soil around them firmly. Give them a good watering as soon as they are planted.

Some of the taller growing herbs such as fennel and sage become naturally dwarfed by the confined root space. They can also be kept in check by light pruning, to make them into good compact bushes.

Suggestions for Small Herb Gardens. The variety in shape and size for a small herb garden is infinite; so much must depend upon the space available.

There are, however, several points to remember, the most important being that – as already mentioned, but necessary to stress – herbs should be grown as close to the kitchen door as possible.

The ideal herb garden for a cook is one which has a paving from the door to the garden and the beds surrounded by paving made from stone, brick or concrete.

Whether the beds are laid out square, round, oblong or hexagonal depends upon the location and number of herbs required. But remember, if you start with four you will soon wish that you had room for eight!

Here is another good idea for a small herb garden. Build up instead of out – quite the fashion after all! For example, an ideal location would be across the corner of a wall or hedge (but not in a shaded corner), or against a bare kitchen wall. In this case, make sure that only the concrete and not the soil touches the wall, so that it cannot absorb any damp. Three tiers built up pyramid fashion, as in the sketch, makes a good and attractive 'garden', allowing a variety of herbs to be tended easily.

A friend of mine, living in a mews cottage in the heart of London, has this type of bed across two-thirds of the front of her cottage, leaving the remaining third for her front door. In it she intersperses such flowers as petunias with the herbs, and very effective it is too.

Suggestions for Large Herb Gardens. A herb border is a popular method of growing herbs in a kitchen garden. I would suggest, for anybody who can, that they go and see the model herb border at the Royal Horticultural Society Garden at Wisley, near Woking in Surrey. Or visit any local herb specialists.

When planting a lot of herbs, it helps tremendously to be able to see the actual plants growing. Some need so much more room for bushing out than others, apart from the different heights to which they grow. See under separate headings for this in the section 'Herbs and How to Grow Them'.

To take but a few examples – rosemary needs to be spaced at least three feet apart, whilst fennel needs twelve to eighteen inches. Marjoram and mint need a foot, whereas chives and the annual summer savory need only six inches.

Herb borders are very attractive planted against a hedge. A herb itself, such as rue or southernwood, may be grown as a hedge, but the aspect must be considered; most herbs need sunshine and light.

The number of plants of each variety must depend upon the size of the family and their taste in food, but be sure to have at least one plant of many varieties so as to try the different fresh flavours.

Herb Lawns

The growing of herb lawns, camomile (chamomile) especially, has become very popular in recent years. Here are a few suggestions on what to grow and how to treat them.

1. **Camomile** *Anthemis nobilis*. This variety of camomile makes an excellent lawn which is hardy enough to keep green even in hot weather. It is also hardy enough to withstand as much wear and tear from walking as an ordinary lawn. Probably few visitors to Buckingham Palace royal garden parties realize that stretches of one of the lawns there are planted with this camomile. It thrives best on light sandy soil, but will grow on anything but clay.

Seeds are sown in the spring, in boxes or special seed beds, and the plants transplanted to the lawn site as soon as they are large enough to handle. Or plants can be bought and planted direct in spring or autumn. They should be planted about four inches apart.

If a thick sward is desired, the lawn should be mowed *regularly* to prevent flowering. The plants should first be 'topped' when they reach three inches. Then the mower should gradually be lowered to about half an inch. The lawn should be weeded and watered until it has become a really thick mat.

2. **Thyme** *Thymus serpyllum*. This is the smallest and hardiest of the thymes and makes a fragrant carpet rather than a strong lawn to walk on. It will not bear much traffic, but smells glorious when trodden upon and crushed. It is really more suitable for growing in a special corner or around a garden seat.

This variety of thyme is also well suited for planting between paving stones, or to make an entire pathway.

It is best planted as established roots in the spring. Keep it well watered and weeded as it takes a little time to settle.

It would be a pity to mow a thyme lawn and so forego the beauty of the bright pinky-mauve flowers, but it *can* be mowed if required.

3. **Pennyroyal** *Mentha requieni*. This is one of the smallest of the mint family and, like thyme, is not really hard enough to bear much traffic. Treat it in the same way as thyme (see *Note* page 20).

Storing Herbs

Drying Herbs

There is absolutely no comparison between the flavour of fresh and dried herbs, but there are times when we have to make do with the dried variety. If they are growing in the garden, it needs only a little time and trouble to dry them successfully.

First, a few points of importance.
1. Keep each herb separate, without any possibility of one becoming mixed with another.
2. Have the storage bottles or jars clean and clearly marked before the herbs are dry and ready for packaging.
3. Do not keep dried herbs in a moist atmosphere, even in airtight containers.

For the drying of leaves, the best time to pick them is as soon as the flower buds appear on the plant, but before they begin to open. At this period, the greatest abundance of natural oils is concentrated in the leaves, which will give the fullest flavour when dried.

Small-leaved herbs, such as thyme, savory and tarragon, can be picked by the branch and hung up to dry in bundles. Larger leaves, such as mint, sage and basil, are better picked separately from the growing branches. Be sure that each leaf is perfect, without spot or blemish.

Pick them in warm dry weather, in the morning after the dew has evaporated and before the sun has become hot enough to draw out the natural oils.

For those tied in bundles, place in a warm dry place such as an airing cupboard, where they can be hung from the slatted shelves and left only until they are dry (brittle) enough to bottle. This should not take more than a few days. A kitchen or bathroom, although warm, is not good because of the steam which occurs in both. If they have to be left in a passage, garage or other location which may be dusty, tie them in a piece of muslin.

The best temperature for the first twenty-four hours is about 90° F. then it can come down to the seventies. Unless the weather is persistently wet, so that the herbs have had to be picked in a moist condition, it is not advisable to dry them in an oven. If this is necessary, the temperature should be kept as low as possible. Neither is it good to dry them in the sun. A dark place allows them to retain their colour more successfully.

When the leaves are dry, strip them off the branches and store in airtight bottles or jars. Or they can be rubbed through a wire sieve.

For the larger leaves, place them on a tray covered with absorbent kitchen paper and dry them at the same temperature. Keep turning them over and around so that they will dry evenly. When they are brittle enough, crush into small pieces before turning into airtight containers, or rub through a wire sieve.

Seeds of herbs for drying should be allowed to dry partially on the stems before collection. Then strip them off and place on paper-covered trays to dry. Keep moving them around so that they dry evenly.

Freezing Herbs

Herbs freeze surprisingly well, but the small rather hard-leaved varieties such as thyme, oregano, rosemary and savory, which dry so well, are really not worth space in a freezer.

Others, such as parsley (which I do not think is good dried), tarragon, chives, basil and mint are well worth freezing.

Chives, which are particularly good frozen, can be frozen whole and then chopped when removed from the freezer. But other soft-leaved herbs are not satisfactory frozen in sprays. They should all be chopped before freezing.

Here's how: if the herb is not perfectly clean, wash it quickly and then gently pat it dry in a cloth.

Chop and pack into small ice cube containers – whatever size you wish. Wrap several of these together in foil or transparent wrapping film. Or wrap each separately. Be careful to mark each herb for easy identification later.

Packets of bouquet garni can be tied together and frozen. Leaving a long piece of string for future use, tie together three or four sprays of parsley (satisfactory for this use), a sprig of thyme, a small bay leaf and any other herbs you may fancy. Make as many as you like, place a piece of polythene between each and then wrap the whole lot together as before. Each bouquet can then be removed individually as required.

Spices and Where They Grow

Allspice (Pimento. Jamaica Pimento. Jamaica Pepper. Clove Pepper) *Pimenta officinalis.* The allspice tree was discovered by some of the early explorers in the Western hemisphere. It grows in the Carribean islands and Central America and, although the tree will grow in other parts of the world, it will not bear fruit anywhere else.

The evergreen tree grows twenty-five to thirty feet in height. The fruit is harvested when mature but still green. After drying, it is dark reddish-brown, round, with a roughish surface and about the size of a pea.

It got its name, allspice, because the aroma and flavour of the seed resembles a combination of cinnamon, clove and nutmeg. But it should not be confused with 'mixed pickling spice' which is a mixture of allspice berries and many other spices.

NOTE: Nor should pimento be confused with pimiento (with an extra i) which is a species of capsicum (green and red sweet peppers, chillis, etc.).

Anise *Pimpinella anisum.* The seeds we use come from an annual herbaceous plant growing to about one foot high. Originally coming from the region East of the Mediterranean, the plants now grow also in Spain, Turkey, Bulgaria, Syria and the United States.

Pliny said of the anise, 'It serves well for seasoning all meats and the kitchen cannot get along without it.'

Many nations also found anise indispensable in the old days. The Assyrians used it as a medicine; the Romans as a digestive at feasts, often ending a big banquet with a cake spiced with aniseed. And many people used it as a charm against bad dreams and the 'evil eye'.

Anise fruits, commonly called aniseed, are tiny, brown and oval, with an unmistakable flavour of liquorice. It is from them that such liqueurs as anisette are made.

Capsicum. Capsicum is a species of herbaceous plant, annual and perennial, of which there are many varieties.

Plant historians believe that they came originally from South America. At all events, Peter Martyr, who went to America with Columbus in 1493, writing of them said that here was 'pepper more pungent than that from Caucasus'.

These capsicums cover a range whose fruit we know by other names. For example, *Chillis* (*Capsicum frutescens* and others), the smallest of the capsicum family which we know as frantically hot. In tropical climates, they are grown and used fresh, particularly in curries. In Europe and temperate climates, they are used dried, or ground as chilli powder, chili (the American spelling) powder, red pepper or cayenne, of which cayenne is traditionally the hottest. It may be orangy red, whereas chilli powder and red pepper are usually a brighter red. They are also sold in flakes as 'crushed red pepper'.

Paprika comes from another species, *Capsicum annuum.* This is known as paprika pepper, which although much the same colour as cayenne and chilli powder, is nothing like as hot. It came originally from the Caribbean region and was first brought to Europe to be grown in Turkey. In the 16th century it was taken to Hungary, whose people so fell in love with the flavour that they created their national dishes around it, calling it Paprika, which means 'Turkish pepper'.

In Europe there are many types of paprika, but in England the usual kind is the 'sweet' type which is a brilliant red colour, so invaluable for garnishing many a dull-coloured dish. Spain also uses this sweet type exclusively.

Then there are sweet pepper flakes which are now sold dried for use in stews. They are the dried flesh of the much larger red and green capsicums, which we know as the vegetable 'sweet peppers'.

Though a vegetable and not a spice, it is worth mentioning that the canned red *Pimiento* (with two i's) is another variety of capsicum.

Caraway *Carum carvi.* Caraway is a biennial plant, reaching a height of about two feet. The seeds, which are used in cooking, have a tendency to shatter when ripe, so they have to be harvested at night or before the dew has dried off them.

It was the Romans who carried the seeds of the caraway, amongst many others, from its home in Asia Minor to the many countries which they conquered, including Britain. In Scotland seed cakes are still known as 'Carvi cakes'.

Now caraway grows happily in northern Europe, particularly Holland.

The seeds are larger than anise seeds, but otherwise look much like them. They also have the same, though stronger, flavour of liquorice. The German name for caraway is 'Kümmel' and the oil from caraway goes into making the famous liqueur of that name.

Cardamom *Elettaria cardamomum*. The perennial bush cardamom plant grows from six to twelve feet high. It is a native of India, but is now grown commercially in India, Ceylon and Guatemala.

It is the second most expensive spice in the world (the first is saffron), because each seed pod has to be snipped off the plant by hand, with a pair of scissors.

The dried and bleached pods, when they reach the public, are buff coloured, three sided and between a quarter and half an inch long. Inside are numerous small black seeds which have a delightfully warm, slightly pungent and highly aromatic flavour.

No wonder they were known as 'Grains of Paradise' and in ancient times were chewed by the Arabs as a confection! To this day, the Arabians' passion for black coffee is renowned and this they often flavour with cardamom, to assuage the bitterness.

The Vikings discovered cardamoms on their travels a thousand or more years ago, and took them back with them to Scandinavia. Since that time, the flavour of cardamom has been a favourite throughout Scandinavia. True Danish pastries, for example, always have a faint aroma of cardamom about them.

Cayenne See Capsicum page 23.

Cinnamon *Cinnamomum zeylanicum* and *Cinnamomum cassia*. The evergreen cinnamon tree is a member of the laurel family and a native of the Far East.

In Ceylon, the trees grow wild in the wet forests up to fifty feet in height. But when cultivated they are kept down to six or eight feet. A slightly different species grows in Indonesia, India, South Vietnam and China.

The pungent sweet flavour, which we know as cinnamon, comes from the dried bark of the tree. This is stripped off and after going through several processes emerges dried and curled into what are known as 'quills' or 'pipes'. These are the sticks of cinnamon which we buy. It is also sold in powder form.

The spice which comes from Ceylon is slightly different in flavour from that which is grown in Indonesia and Vietnam. And it is from these countries that America imports and exports its cinnamon spice, preferring the flavour to the Ceylonese variety.

Cinnamon is one of the first spices to have been used and enjoyed by man. Not only was it used as a flavouring for food, but also as a medicine, a favourite perfume and as one of the aromatics burned as incense in the temples of the gods.

The Egyptians imported cinnamon nearly 2000 years B.C. It was mentioned in the Bible. Wealthy Romans luxuriated in cinnamon-scented baths. Mediaeval magicians always kept cinnamon on hand and it was one of the ingredients in their 'love-potions'.

Cinnamon was the lure of Ceylon's conquerors, so valuable was the spice trade in those days. The Portuguese monopolized the trade there, from 1505–1658. Then the Dutch took over until 1696; during their occupation, the penalty for the illegal sale of a single stick of cinnamon was death. From 1696 when the British ousted the Dutch, they ran the cinnamon industry which for centuries had been Ceylon's greatest source of wealth.

To this day, the flavour of cinnamon and the scent from it are used in great quantity by people around the world. It is one of the essential components of many mixtures of spices, both sweet and savoury.

Cloves *Eugenia aromatica*. The clove tree is a beautiful evergreen which grows up to a height of forty feet. It is a native of the Moluccas or Spice Islands, but is now grown commercially in Tanzania (Zanzibar), in most of the West Indian islands, Indonesia, Malagasy Republic (Madagascar), and in other hot climates.

It is said that nutmegs have to smell the sea and the clove has to see it. At all events from early accounts, the original clove-covered small islands were a beautiful sight, with the deep green trees covered with tiny brilliant red flowers. And the fragrance which wafted out to the ships, told the sailors that they had arrived at the 'Garden of Spices' – in other words the Moluccas.

But the clove we use is the dried unopened flower bud, like a little round ball on the end of the stem. As the buds have to be picked at this stage for drying, the beauty and scent of the opened blossoms has to be sacrificed.

The name clove is derived from the Latin word *clavus*, a nail, which the half inch long dried clove so resembles.

It takes 4000 to 7000 dried clove buds to make one pound of spice, so naturally they commanded a price commensurate with their rarity. And down the centuries there have been bloody battles for the control of both the islands where they grew, and the European markets where they were sold. Portugal, Holland and Great Britain were, as usual, the great contenders for this prize.

In ancient times, cloves, the clove flowers and the oil, were used for decoration, perfume and love-potions, rather than for flavouring food. It was used as a flavouring for medicines, however. The Arabs used it 2000 years ago to alleviate the bitterness of their fever medicines. And in the 3rd century B.C., one of the Han Emperors of China ordered his courtiers to hold cloves in their mouths while in his presence!

Coriander *Coriandrum sativum*. Coriander is a herb growing to about two feet, but it is the seed which is used as a spice and therefore it is included in the list of spices. The seed should not be picked from the plant until it is ripe, and should then be dried off thoroughly. The green seed has a rather unpleasant taste.

Coriander seeds have been found in Egyptian tombs of 960 B.C. It is known to have grown in Persia 3000 years ago and also to have been grown in the Hanging Gardens of Babylon.

It was mentioned several times in the Old Testament, as for example Exodus 16, 31 says, 'And the house of Israel called the name thereof Manna; and it was like coriander seed, white; and the taste of it was like wafers made with honey.' And again in Numbers 11, 7 and 8, 'And the manna was as coriander seed, and the colour thereof as the colour of bdellium.

'And the people went about, and gathered it, and ground it in mills, or beat it in a mortar, and baked it in pans, and made cakes of it: and the taste of it was as the taste of fresh oil.'

Pliny, in the first century, wrote that the finest coriander seeds came from Egypt. Today, they are still an essential spice for flavouring food in India, China, the Arab world and Mexico. In the United States and Great Britain, it is included in sausages of various kinds, meat products and liquors.

Cumin (also spelt Cummin, Comino seed) **Jeera** (in India and the East) *Cuminum cyminum*. Cumin, or jeera, is a small annual plant which was a native of the Nile Valley, but for centuries has been cultivated in India, Africa, Morocco, China, Malta, Sicily, Palestine, Lebanon, the United States, Latin America and the Mediterranean area. So it is a popular spice.

Cumin has many superstitions associated with it and is mentioned in the Bible. In Matthew 23, 23 Jesus said, 'Woe unto you, scribes and Pharisees, hypocrites! for ye pay tithe of mint and anise and cummin and have omitted the weightier matters of the law . . .'

Cumin seed looks like anise, dill and caraway seeds, but has a strong aromatic flavour unlike any of them. Pliny considered it the best of all the condiments. And I find I am in strong agreement with Pliny! I seldom make a curry without adding an extra quantity of cumin seeds.

It was written about exclusively in the Middle Ages by herbal writers. Now it is an essential ingredient in curry powder, and in America's chili powder. It is also used liberally in Near and Middle Eastern and Latin American cooking. The Scandinavians, Dutch and Swiss use it in cheeses, and the Germans use it in pork and sauerkraut dishes.

Curry powder. In India and Ceylon, curry powder is ground freshly each day by housewives and profes-sional cooks alike, from a variety of spices. Each person varies the number and quantity of the spices they use. The flavours and heat are also varied according to the type of food to be curried.

Commercial curry powder is a mixture of anything from twelve to twenty different spices. The heat of each variety varies considerably from relatively mild to extremely hot, according to the amount of ground chillis included.

When making a real Eastern curry, it is interesting to add spices whose flavour you like particularly, to any standard mixture. For example, I rarely make a curry (not a curry sauce) without the addition of turmeric and jeera (cumin) seeds. These seem to give a more authentic flavour of the southern Indian curries I knew so well.

From Indian shops in Britain and the United States, it is also possible to buy garam masala – a mixture of spices without heat – to mix with curry powder, if sufficient of the different spices are not stocked to mix your own.

Fenugreek *Trigonella foenum-graecum*. Fenugreek, also known as 'Greek Hay Seed' or 'Methi' in the East, is an annual herb growing to a height of about two feet.

It is indigenous to south-eastern Europe, but has been grown in India, Egypt, Morocco and the Lebanon for centuries.

Fenugreek is a little known spice these days, yet the ground seeds are one of the essential spices in curry powder. The herb was used in ancient times as a medicine and the whole plant given to cattle as fodder.

Ginger *Zingiber officinale*. Ginger is an herbaceous perennial consisting of an underground stem, or rhizome, from which leafy shoots grow up to three feet in height.

Native of India and China, it was one of the first true Oriental spices to make its way westward. Now it is grown in other tropical climates such as West Africa, Jamaica, the West Indies and Central America.

Ginger was for centuries the rich man's spice, together with peppercorns. It is woven into romantic legends of all sorts, the flowers also having an irresistible perfume.

It is said to have been discovered in Greece as delicious for gingerbread almost 5000 years ago; fancy gingerbread was a great favourite of Queen Elizabeth I and her court.

But it is the Chinese cuisine which uses ginger in all its forms, as the most important single flavouring for its incomparable food.

Ginger is sold in many forms. From some sources it is peeled, some unpeeled. Most countries growing it for export, classify it into several grades. It can be bought freshly preserved or 'green', and this is the best flavour for savoury dishes. These pieces of rhizome (root) are found in Oriental shops. They look dried, but when peeled are a greeny-cream colour, juicy and very hot. They can be kept wrapped tightly in foil in a refrigerator for many weeks, and in a freezer for many months. Ginger can also be bought in small cans already peeled and called 'Green Ginger' on the can. This is delicious for Chinese dishes of all kinds and is not quite as hot as the fresh root.

Ginger is also sold completely dried and very hard. It is the type used for pickling and is always an ingredient in pickling spice. This can be softened by soaking it in cold water overnight.

Ground, it is sold in powder form which can be stored in an airtight container indefinitely.

Crystallized and preserved ginger are made from fresh roots and are considered confections rather than spices.

Juniper *Juniperus communis.* The Juniper tree is a small evergreen which is a native to Europe, the Arctic and northern parts of Africa.

In the past, there were many legends concerning its power of magic and its holiness; possibly because the berries are stimulating for the appetite and digestion and thought to be cleansing for the blood. Also they have a disinfectant quality when the berries are burned. This is why, during the last century, they were used in winter in Switzerland to sweeten the air in schools, whose windows had to be kept closed against the cold. They are also sometimes used to clean the air in the room of an invalid.

They are popular for smoking some kinds of meat, and are used greatly in Scandinavia and on the Continent for flavouring different kinds of food.

The berries take two to three years to ripen on the tree, then they are picked and dried. They should be crushed (with the back of a spoon) before use and used with care since they have a strong taste. They make a particularly good flavouring for strong and rich foods such as game, hare, venison and pork.

Juniper berries also provide the flavouring in the manufacture of gin.

Mace See Nutmeg.

Mustard, Black or Brown *Brassica nigra.* **White or Yellow** *Brassica sinapsis alba.* There are two kinds of mustard grown as a spice; commonly known as black or brown and white or yellow. Both are herbaceous annual plants which came originally from Europe and south-east Asia, but are now grown extensively for export in the United Kingdom, Denmark, Canada and the United States.

Mustard as a titillating spice has been known to man since prehistoric times. It got its name of 'mustard' from a corruption of 'must-seeds'. When the Romans occupied Britain, they mixed the crushed seeds with 'must' – the newly pressed juice from grapes before fermentation sets in.

The seeds dropping from the plants grow all too easily and so can become quite a weed pest. There is a nice legend in this connection however. When the Padres were crossing California on their famous Mission Trail, they planted mustard seeds along the way so that on their return they could follow the conspicuous yellow plants. Perhaps the later popular children's game of paper chase has originated from this episode.

Unlike other spices, the seeds and even the crushed powder, have no scent whatever. It is only when the enzyme activity is started by the addition of liquid that mustard develops its pungent character. It can be mixed into a paste with water, white wine or vinegar.

It would be impossible to describe mustard better than did novelist Anatole France who said 'A tale without love is like beef without Mustard: an insipid dish.'

Nutmeg and Mace *Myristica fragrans.* The bushy nutmeg tree grows up to thirty to forty feet in height and is said to like to 'smell the sea'. At all events it is certainly an island plant, a native of the Moluccas, but is now cultivated also in Indonesia, and on the island of Penang in Malaya.

The fruit, when ripe, resembles a peach in appearance. In some places the fruit are allowed to fall and are collected every morning, whilst in others they are collected off the tree by means of a long pronged stick with a basket attached.

The outer husk is removed first and some of this is preserved in syrup and looked upon as a delicacy in the Netherlands Indies. Then the bright red lacy aril or fruit fibre – the mace – can be seen surrounding the little brown nutmeg.

The mace and nutmeg are both dried slowly. The mace is often ground on the spot and only a small quantity is exported as 'blades' of mace. The nutmeg, on the other hand, is usually exported as a whole nut and is then ground by manufacturers as required for their trade.

Nutmeg and mace were not known in European history before A.D. 600 and it was not until the Dutch had cornered the spice trade in the Moluccas, in the 16th century, that these two powerful and wonderful spices became really well known.

It is interesting that the highest trained French chefs use nutmeg and mace in their cooking far more than any of the heartier, stronger spices. These two blend well with the blander flavours of the classical French cuisine, which uses home grown herbs for its extra seasoning. France had little to do with the battles for the spice trade in past centuries, as her ships and her mariners appear not to have been as intrepid or adventurous as those of the Portuguese, Dutch and British. Therefore spices were not in common use in France.

The Dutch on the other hand, whose fleets and men controlled much of the East Indies with its spice trade, use spices a lot and herbs much less in their cooking. To this day, their vegetables usually appear with a sprinkling of nutmeg.

Pepper *Piper nigrum.* The pepper plant is a perennial climbing vine which grows wild up trees to a height of twenty to twenty-five feet, but when it is cultivated it is kept down to not more than fifteen feet.

It is a truly tropical plant, growing only within about ten degrees of the Equator, and is now grown and exported mainly from India, Ceylon, Indonesia, Malaysia and Brazil.

The peppercorns we know grow in racemes, like grapes, but not so close to each other. As the berries ripen, they turn from green to yellow to red. Those destined for sale as black pepper are picked when they are still slightly underripe. As they dry, the colour changes to black and this outer hull is left on. It gives a more pungent flavour than white pepper.

White pepper is the fully ripe berry, soaked soon after picking to soften the outer hull. This can then be rubbed off easily, leaving the smooth parchment coloured cone with its milder flavour.

Both black and white should be used in cooking according to the type and colour of the dish. But there is no substitute for the freshly ground black peppercorns from a pepper mill, whenever the dish warrants its use. One of London's most distinguished chefs whom I know well as a kind, good tempered man, gives all his younger under chefs a pepper mill each. If they lose their mill and are found not using one he gets really angry; 'No chef can call himself a chef without using a pepper mill,' he roars!

And how right he is. Every meal has its quota of pepper; for pepper and salt are the twins which improve every savoury dish of any kind. Unlike salt, pepper is not essential to life itself, only to the aesthetic pleasure of eating.

Gerard in his great 'Herball' finished his description of pepper thus: 'All pepper heateth, provoketh, digesteth, draweth, disperseth, and cleanseth the dimness of the sight, as Dioscorides noteth.'

The history of pepper is one of the most romantic of all the spices (see History page 5). The Greeks are known to have been using it as early as the 4th century B.C. As it had then, and for many centuries thereafter, to come to Europe by caravan from the Far East over the most dangerous and tortuous routes, the cost of pepper was prohibitive. So precious was it, that it was used as money – taxes and tributes, ransoms and dowries were paid with it. In the 10th century, English landlords asked for a rent tax of one pound of pepper a year.

This should not be confused with the 'peppercorn rent'. This term is used in modern times to signify a nominal rent, presumably because the size of a peppercorn is so small. The object of such a rent is to secure the acknowledgment by the tenant of the landlord's right over the building or land.

The quest for pepper was one of the reasons why the Portuguese sought and found the sea route around the Cape of Good Hope: after which the cost of pepper in Europe began to drop tremendously. And now we can all use pepper with as much freedom as we like and it deserves.

Poppy seeds *Papaver somniferum.* This is the opium poppy, an annual which can grow as high as four feet, but usually only to two to three feet. The plant came originally from the Mediterranean area, but is now widely cultivated. The best seeds, however, come from Holland.

The deep blue-black poppy seeds sold commercially should be genuine blue poppy seeds, but are sometimes white ones coloured blue artificially. This dye is water soluble, so a few seeds soaked in water will soon tell you whether they are genuine or not.

Although opium and other narcotics are obtained from this plant, there is no need to worry about the seeds. They contain NO narcotic. The seeds cannot form until after the plant has matured to the point where it has lost all of its opium content.

They have been used as a stimulant for the appetite since the Stone Age, some say; others, that mixed with wine and honey, the seeds were used as a regular part of the diet training for the competitors in the original Olympic Games at Olympia. And they also featured on the dining tables of the ancient Romans.

Today, they are used crushed and mixed with sugar and syrup as fillings for pastries and cakes. A poppy grinder is a common enough gadget in a European kitchen.

To crush the seeds without the special grinder, they should be soaked in water for several hours, then crushed between paper with a rolling pin or bottle. Toasting whole seeds in a heavy frying pan over a very gentle heat, or in the oven, brings the flavour out.

Saffron *Crocus sativus.* The spice saffron comes from the stigmas of the mauve flowering autumn crocus. Each crocus has only three stigmas which must be picked by hand; it takes two hundred and twenty-five thousand stigmas to make one pound of spice. This makes it the world's most expensive spice. Fortunately, a little goes a long way.

The saffron crocus is a native of Asia and of the

Mediterranean area and now is exported chiefly from Spain and Portugal. In both these countries, naturally, it is used extensively in cooking.

Saffron has been written and sung about from ancient times. King Solomon grew it in his gardens. Cleopatra used it in some of her favourite cosmetics. We are told in 'The Bible as History' that the garments of the Children of Israel owed their brightness to natural dyes: saffron for yellow, madder-root for red and the murex snail for purple. Homer sang of the 'saffron-robed morn'.

In the 15th century, those who were caught adulterating saffron were even burned at the stake. In India, the colour of saffron signifies courage and sacrifice, and the Buddhist monks wear saffron coloured robes.

It is thought to have been introduced into England by the returning Crusaders. However, it was cultivated commercially in the light rich soil in the Walden area and the town, Saffron Walden in Essex, got its prefix 'Saffron' from this industry. The town accumulated riches from the demand for saffron as a dye, a medicine and as a spice. But when the cheaper foreign saffron began to be imported in the 18th century, the industry died out altogether.

The dried stigmas are usually sold in tiny packets. Before use, they should be crushed in a pestle and mortar (no Spanish kitchen is without one), and dissolved in water (preferably hot) or milk, or whatever liquid is being used in the dish.

For certain dishes saffron is indispensable. For example, the classical French Bouillabaisse from Marseilles, Spanish Paella and Arroz con Pollo and England's Cornish Saffron Cakes.

Sesame (also called 'Benne' or 'Bene' seed) *Sesamum indicum*. Sesame is an annual herb which grows up to four feet. The mature pods are apt to burst at the touch scattering the small white seeds, which makes harvesting by machinery difficult. But so valuable are the seeds for their high protein and mineral oil content, that new strains of the plant are being tried and grown to eliminate this hazard.

Sesame really seems to have been the Father of spices, since Assyrian mythology has the ancient gods drinking sesame wine before they created the earth! Then Yama, God of Death, is said to have given his blessing to it for various uses, including funerals and expiatory ceremonies, as a purifier and a symbol of immortality.

Countless nations have used it, and still do as oil: in their medicines, in cosmetics – like Cleopatra who is said to have used the oil as a skin beautifier (and she should have known) – and in their food. Neither must we forget the famous Arabian, Ali Baba, who said 'Open Sesame' to reveal that glittering jewel-filled cave!

In the Middle East, sesame paste, called 'tahini', is used extensively in cooking. It can be bought in health food stores, or at grocers specialising in Greek, Lebanese or Syrian products.

Turmeric *Curcuma longa*. Turmeric is an herbaceous, perennial plant of the ginger family, whose leaves grow to about two feet high. But, like ginger, it is the rootstock or rhizome which is used as a spice.

It has been known in the Orient for thousands of years, but has been a much neglected spice in the Occident. Dried and ground, the spice is bright orange in colour and in cooking can be interchanged with saffron for both colour and flavour. To my mind it has a much more attractive taste than saffron and I always use it in preference.

Turmeric is an essential ingredient of curry powder and, together with cumin seed, I find a bit extra adds that little something to curries. It is also the spice used with mustard in mustard pickles and sauce.

Turmeric grows in so many countries in the Orient, West Indies and South America, and is used as a most versatile spice for flavouring, perfumery, dyeing and the chemical industry, that it is difficult to know from where or how it actually originated. At all events, it is an Oriental spice par excellence, which deserves to be known and used far more widely in the West.

Vanilla *Vanilla planifolia*. Vanilla might be called the 'Queen of Seasonings', coming as it does from rare and beautiful pale yellow orchids. These orchids grow in clusters of a dozen or more blossoms, which flower usually for not more than one day.

The vanilla vine is a native of tropical America, particularly Mexico, although it is now cultivated also in Madagascar, the Seychelles, Java, Tahiti and other tropical areas.

The fruit, or vanilla bean, is similar in many respects to the familiar string or green bean – but with an exquisite flavour. For it makes sweet sweeter and has the propensity of coaxing out the flavour of such commodities as chocolate, coffee and fruit.

When harvested, the bean is green in colour and is completely odourless and flavourless. It takes up to six months of careful and skillful labour in curing, fermenting and drying, to produce the dark brown, nearly black colour, and the characteristic fragrance. The oil distilled from the bean and so widely used, is called 'vanillin'.

The history of vanilla dates back to long before the Aztec reign in Mexico, but goodness knows who first discovered its marvellous potential.

It was brought to fame by the Spanish adventurer Hernando Cortéz who, in 1560, went to the palace of the Aztec King – Montezuma. There, Cortéz was served a delectable beverage which the King called 'Xoco-Lath', made from the powdered bean of the cocoa tree (chocolate) and flavoured with what the Aztecs called 'Tlilxochitl', meaning 'black pod'.

This beverage seems to have been a cross between a drink and a sweet; for the froth was prepared in such a way that it was almost solid enough to be eaten. In fact, Montezuma had it served in golden goblets with spoons of gold or finely wrought tortoiseshell. So fond was he of this concoction, that he had fifty served to him each day; two thousand was the daily order for his palace!

When Cortéz took the priceless Aztec treasure of gold and silver back to Spain, he also took some black pods, which the Spaniards called 'vanilla', meaning 'little scabbard'. This proved almost as valuable as the treasure of precious metals.

We buy bottles of vanilla essence and probably use it without much thought. But it is important for the true flavour of vanilla to buy the pure essence distilled from the bean itself, NOT the synthetic essence.

The inimitable flavour of vanilla can best be enjoyed to the full by using the bean, either in an infusion if liquid is called for, or as vanilla sugar.

The bean can be rinsed, dried and used many times before the flavour begins to recede; one pod will last at least four to six weeks.

For an infusion, the liquid should be brought to the boil and the vanilla bean dropped in as the pan is removed from the heat. Then allow ten to thirty minutes infusion, depending upon the strength of flavour required.

For vanilla sugar, fill a bottle with castor sugar and according to the size, push in one or two beans. Or cut one bean in half lengthways – this works faster. Leave well screwed down for the flavour to permeate the sugar. Remember that vanilla sugar is sweeter than plain sugar, so use carefully.

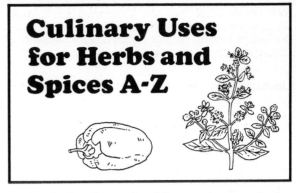

Culinary Uses for Herbs and Spices A-Z

In the food industry the difference between herbs, spices and condiments is given as follows:

Herbs are classified as soft stemmed aromatic plants whose herbaceous tops are gathered. They are used fresh or, when dried, the leaves are usually rubbed off the hard stalks.

Many of these plants grow wild in temperate climates, especially around the Mediterranean area and in the United States of America, Mexico and Canada, where they are now grown commercially in enormous quantities.

Spices are dried aromatic vegetable products, usually only parts of plants such as roots, bark, flower buds, fruits and seeds. They grow in a variety of tropical countries.

Condiments are also spices, except salt, and are usually added to food on the table, or after cooking.

To these should be added those composite spices and herbs, which have been pioneered in America and are now sold in Britain and many other countries. For example, Apple Pie Spice – a mixture amongst others, of cinnamon, nutmeg and sugar; Pumpkin Pie Spice – cinnamon, ginger, nutmeg, cloves and so on; Meat Tenderizer – salt, papain (from papaw fruit), etc.; Barbecue Seasoning – a mixture of spices, dextrose, monosodium glutamate and liquid smoke flavour; Italian Seasoning – a mixture of six or seven herbs; and countless others.

Also the important composite condiments such as Seasoned Salt – a mixture of sixteen or seventeen ingredients such as spices, sugar, monosodium glutamate, onion and herbs mixed with the salt; Seasoned Pepper – with sweet peppers, spices, sugar, lactic acid, etc.; Hickory Smoked Salt; and so on.

Monosodium Glutamate is described in the Dictionary of Nutrition and Food Technology as: 'Glutamate, Sodium. Sodium salt of the amino acid, glutamic acid. Enhances the flavour of some foods, especially meat and vegetables, apparently by stimulating the taste buds. Commercially manufactured from sugar beet pulp and wheat gluten. Glutamic acid has two acidic groups and it is the monosodium salt, known as MSG, that has this flavour property. First introduced as a flavouring agent under the Japanese name of "Ajinomoto".'

Monosodium glutamate has in itself no nutritional value.

General Points to remember for the use of herbs and spices in cooking are:

1. Every herb and spice begins to lose its potency directly it is cut, so whenever possible buy little and often. Keep in airtight containers and away from a damp atmosphere.

2. The flavour of herbs and spices grown in different parts of the world varies considerably, so when buying the dried varieties, particularly spices, it is better not to try to economise but buy those which come from the best areas.

In any case, the art of flavouring in cooking is to use *just* sufficient to enhance the subtlety of a dish, and not to drown the inherent flavour of the food.

3. Ground spices give out their flavour quickly, so for any long cooking dishes such as soups and stews, add them only for the last 20 minutes or so of cooking.

4. Use at least twice the quantity of fresh herbs as dried herbs to give the same intensity of flavour. But the actual flavour of the fresh herb far outstrips that of its dried self.

5. Different herbs and spices have an affinity with certain types of food. Try the recommended combinations first, then experiment with any others you may fancy.

A survey carried out by one of the world's largest spice houses says, 'Few women know how to use spices and herbs, and therefore fear them. Yet it can be the difference between good and bad cooking.'

The favourite dozen herbs and spices amongst home cooks, from a survey by one of the largest British food manufacturers from cookery editors, is given as: nutmeg, cinnamon, bay leaves, cloves, ginger, marjoram, rosemary, sage, thyme, paprika, mixed spice, tarragon.

Culinary Uses for Herbs

Balm. Leaves have a lemony flavour. Use in summer drinks, iced tea, fruit salad; mix with other herbs when a light lemon flavour is desired.

Basil. Slightly clove pepper flavour. Use leaves in all tomato dishes; egg dishes; potato, rice, bean and other vegetable salads; French dressing; vinegar; bean, pea, beef and game soups; fish and shellfish; sauces for pasta; lamb, venison, game, beef and veal stews; aubergines; courgettes.

Bay leaves. Use in bouquet garni; stock; fish and meat stews; boiled beef, gammon, pickled pork, tongue and poultry; pot roasts; marinade for meats; sauces; milk puddings.

Borage. Light cucumber flavour. Use leaves and flowers in sprays to garnish beverages; punch, claret cups, Pimm's No. 1. Young leaves with potatoes, cottage cheese, fish salads. Flowers can be crystallized.

Bouquet garni. The classic bouquet garni is composed of a small bay leaf, three to four sprays of parsley including the stalks and a sprig of thyme – all tied in a piece of muslin for extraction before serving. To these can be added any other herb, which may be required for any particular dish.

Burnet. Flavour resembles cucumber. Mixes well with tarragon and rosemary. Use leaves for green salads, cream and cottage cheese; spiced vinegars.

Chervil. Slight anise flavour. Use leaves in salads; omelettes and egg dishes; soups and as a soup; cream sauces; mixes well with other herbs and is one of the essential herbs for the French 'fines herbes'.

Chives. Mild onion flavour. Use chopped leaves with salads of all kinds; cream and cottage cheese; omelettes and egg dishes; cream sauces; mashed and baked potatoes; as a garnish for cream soups; mixed with chopped parsley and chervil particularly.

Dill. Slight anise flavour. *Sprays* and *leaves* used as garnish for cucumber and fish dishes; open sandwiches; pickling; vegetables, particularly marrow, tomatoes, carrots, beetroot, cabbage, turnips, courgettes, mushrooms; salads; sauces for fish; soups. *Seeds* used in pickles; fish dishes; grilled lamb and pork; stews; cheese dishes; sauerkraut; cabbage and cauliflower.

Fennel. Slight anise flavour. Similar to dill in every respect, but even better for fish, particularly oily fish. Use in exactly the same way as dill. *Seeds* are excellent for a fish court bouillon.

Garlic. More pungent than onion. For chopping and crushing use a plate, or a board kept solely for garlic. Or use a garlic press. Use in meat and fish stews; roast lamb; hamburgers; salads; French dressing; pasta dishes; baked and buttered beans; vegetable dishes; spinach; cheese dishes; garlic bread.

Horseradish. Strong hot flavour like mustard. Use roots grated, minced or ground as a sauce with cream, in sauces, beef dishes, shellfish dishes.

Hyssop. Slightly bitter minty flavour. Use leaves and tender tops in stuffings; stews; salads; soups; oily fish such as eel; herb tea; fruit cocktails, particularly cranberry; fruit pies.

Lovage. Flavour like celery but harsher. Use stems like celery; can be candied like angelica. Use *leaves* and *seeds* in place of celery for soups, stews, salads and for any dish to replace celery, but use sparingly.

Marjoram. Sweet spicy flavour. Very versatile in cooking. Use leaves with all meat dishes and stews; poultry; stuffings; vegetables, particularly potatoes, carrot, cabbage, celery, runner beans; salads; soups; fish sauces; cheese dishes; egg dishes.

Mint. Strong spearmint flavour. Use leaves in vinegar as a sauce for lamb; mint jelly, mint vinegar; grilled lamb and veal chops; stuffings; peas; new potatoes; carrots; salads; tea.

Apple Mint. Distinct flavour of apple with overtones of mint. Said by some to be superior to spearmint for mint sauce. Use also as garnish for beverages, fruit cups, teas, fruit salads and salads.

Peppermint. Strong flavour of peppermint. Use leaves for sauces, jellies, fruit cups, salads and vegetables.

Onion, Welsh. Onions themselves are not as strong flavoured as shallots. Use in place of onion in the same manner. *Leaves* resemble chives in looks, but flavour is very weak. Use in place of chives in winter, if chives are unprocurable.

Oregano. Stronger and more pungent flavour than marjoram. Use leaves with pasta and all Italian dishes, particularly spaghetti Bolognese and pizza; chili con carne; meat, rabbit and stuffings.

Parsley. Our most versatile herb with its own distinctive flavour. *Stalks* contain stronger flavour than the leaves, so use in stews and stocks; whole sprays for bouquet garni. *Leaves* used in cream sauces, especially for broad beans; vegetables; fish; tongue; ham; salads; omelettes and egg dishes; soups; as garnish for vegetables of every kind and any savoury dish which needs colour.

Pennyroyal. Peppermint flavour and more pungent than other mints. Leaves used as garnish for beverages and tea; chopped for garnish in place of mint.

Rosemary. Delicate distinctive flavour. Use *leaves* or *sprigs* stuck into joints of roast lamb, veal and inside chicken. Or lay them in the roasting tin, or in a casserole for pot roasting, and remove before serving. Use chopped in rabbit dishes; stews; vegetable dishes, particularly marrow, potatoes, peas; stuffings; soups; fish.

Rue. Rather bitter flavour. Use leaves sparingly in salads, salad sandwiches and medicinal tea.

Sage. Strong distinctive flavour. Use leaves for stuffings, especially pork, goose, duck; sausage dishes; meat loaves; pea soup; biscuit pastry for meat pies; cheese; tea.

Savory. Summer savory has a more delicate flavour than winter savory. Both have a peppery taste; the winter variety being quite strong, so use with care. Use *sprigs* for boiling with broad beans and all kinds of green beans; chopped *leaves* in a sauce for beans, tomatoes, fish; poultry; stews; pork and veal chops; salads; pickled cucumbers; biscuit pastry for meat and vegetable pies.

Sorrel. Slightly bitter flavour. Leaves used for salad with lettuce; as a vegetable mixed with spinach and lettuce; as a soup mixed with spinach, lettuce or cabbage.

Southernwood. Rather bitter flavour. Young leaves used in salads and sparingly in cakes.

Sweet Cicely. Sweetish flavour faintly resembling anise. Use *leaves* and crushed *seeds* in cordials; fruit cups; fruit salads; stewed tart fruit such as rhubarb, gooseberries, currants, plums, damsons. Use fresh leaves, chopped, when a faint anise flavour is desired in salads, soups, fish and root vegetables. A specially good herb mixed with other herbs.

Tarragon. Liquorice and slightly bitter flavour. Leaves used for tarragon vinegar; chicken; kidneys; sweetbreads; in 'fines herbes'; sauces for fish; sauces Béarnaise, Tartare, Verte; tarragon butter for shellfish and vegetables, particularly mushrooms, courgettes, artichokes, tomatoes, beetroot, cabbage, broccoli; cold egg dishes.

Thyme. Common thyme has a distinctive strong flavour. Lemon thyme is less strong and has a lemony flavour. Use *sprigs* of either for bouquet garni and stock. *Leaves* in stuffings for chicken, turkey, veal, rabbit; stews; soups; salads; vegetables, particularly beetroots, aubergines, onions, carrots, tomatoes; meat loaves; fish dishes.

Culinary Uses for Spices

Allspice. Flavour resembles a mixture of cinnamon, cloves and nutmeg. Use *whole* berries (usually tied in muslin) in pickles; stews; meat broth; boiled fish. Use *ground* in gingerbread; fruit cakes; black bun; steamed dried fruit puddings; soups; tomatoes; relishes and chutneys.

Anise Seed. Liquorice flavour. Use seeds *whole* in biscuits and cookies; cakes; scattered over rolls; in milk drinks and puddings; green and red cabbage; carrots; meat stews.

Capsicums. See under Chillis page 23 and Paprika page 23.

Caraway. Distinct liquorice flavour, stronger than anise. Use seeds *whole* in rye and other breads; cakes; pickles; sauerkraut; cabbage, white and red; turnips; pork; liver; meat stews.

Cardamom. Distinctive warm, slightly pungent aromatic flavour. Use seeds *whole* in savoury rice dishes; pickles; curries; coffee. Use *ground* in Danish pastries; buns; coffee cake; Indian sweets; baked apples; pumpkin pie; scattered over melon.

Cayenne. See Capsicums page 23. Cayenne pepper is traditionally the hottest of all spices. An essential ingredient of curries and curry powder. Use in devilled sauces; devilled meats, particularly kidneys, chicken, turkey; meat dishes; fish and shellfish; eggs; vegetable dishes; cheese dishes.

Chilli Powder. See Capsicums page 23. Chilli (spelt with two l's) powder in India and other tropical countries means the powder ground from the small very hot chillis. Chili (spelt with one l) powder, the American condiment, is a blend of spices which combines others with the basic ground chillis. It is not quite as hot as cayenne and is used extensively for Mexican dishes; cocktail sauces for shellfish; minced meat. It is interchangeable with cayenne.

Cinnamon. A pungent sweet spicy flavour. Use *sticks* in cooked apples; prunes; oranges; in spiced fruit for serving with poultry; rice dishes; spiced wine cups; pickling vinegars. Use *ground* in cakes; buns and cookies; fruit pies; vegetables; meat; cinnamon toast; for topping milk and custard puddings.

Cloves. Sharp, spicy, strong flavour. Use *whole* for studding baked ham; for boiling beef; apple and bread sauce; stuck into an onion for sauce and soup making; baked and stewed fruit; pickling fruit; punch and mulled ale. Use *ground* in spiced cakes; mincemeat; buns and cookies; in hot chocolate; chocolate cake; fruit pies; meat stews; beetroot and sweet potatoes.

Coriander. Described as resembling many flavours. Mixture of orange, anise and cumin, is probably as good as any. Use seeds *whole* in pickling; rice dishes; curries and pickled fish. Use *ground* in curry powder; meat stews; roast pork; stuffings; pea soup; lentil dishes; fish dishes; cakes; cookies; milk puddings; custard; Eastern sweets.

Cumin (Jeera). Strong, aromatic, distinctive flavour. Use seeds *whole* in curries; meat stews; Mexican dishes; sauerkraut. Use *ground* in curry powder; sauces; pickles and chutneys; soups; Mexican and Turkish dishes; meat loaves; pork dishes; rice dishes; dried bean dishes; cheese and fish dishes.

Curry Powder. Strength and heat varies. Use in curries; curry sauces; a pinch is excellent in soups and sauces for fish, egg, cheese and vegetable dishes.

Fenugreek. Strong flavour with a background of bitterness. Use *ground* in curries; pickles and chutneys; meat stews.

Ginger. Strong hot flavour. Use *fresh* (*green*) or from cans in Chinese meat and fish dishes; curries; stews; fish dishes. Use *whole dried* pieces in pickles and chutneys; pickling vinegar; ginger beer and wine. Use *ground* in gingerbread; cakes; biscuits and cookies; meat dishes; pickles and chutneys; sauces; soups; vegetables; sweets; puddings; stewed fruit and pies.

Juniper Berries. Strong, bitter-sweet, rather astringent flavour. Use berries crushed with venison; game; hare; pork; braised pigeon and hearts; pâtés; in stuffings for poultry, duck and geese; sauerkraut; cabbage.

Mace. Strong, sweet, slightly bitter flavour, similar to nutmeg but a trifle more snappy. Use *blades* in pickling; rice dishes; hot punches and fruit cups. Use *ground* in fish and shellfish dishes; veal stews; sauces; fruit cakes; pastries.

Mustard. Strong, hot, pungent flavour. Use seeds *whole* in pickling; pickles and chutneys; boiled beetroot. Use *ground* for flavouring meats; poultry; devilled dishes; sauces; egg dishes; cheese dishes; any food which needs pepping up.

Nutmeg. Strong, sweet, slightly bitter aromatic flavour, similar to mace but not as strong. Use grated — either fresh from the nut or bought ground — over milk puddings; custards; junket; cauliflower, spinach, carrots and other vegetables; in cakes; puddings; eggnogs; pies; sauces; fish dishes; in any mixture of spices.

Pepper. Black pepper has a strong, hot, more pungent flavour than white pepper. Use *whole* peppercorns in pickling (often tied in muslin); boiled beef, mutton and gammon; in peppermills to grind at home. Use *ground* in every savoury dish which needs flavouring. Black for dark coloured foods and white for pale coloured foods.

Poppy Seeds. Delightful crunchy, nutty flavour. Use seeds *whole* for toppings on rolls; breads; cakes; cookies; pastries; cheese canapés; salads; buttered noodles. Use *crushed*, mixed with sugar and syrup or honey, as filling for pastries; cakes.

Saffron. Pleasantly bitter, distinctive flavour. Use as described (see page 45) in Paella; chicken and rice dishes; fish dishes; Bouillabaisse and other soups; curries; rice; breads and cakes.

Sesame Seeds. Crisp nut-like flavour. Use *untoasted* scattered over breads; rolls; cookies; scones. Use *toasted* (to a pale brown like poppy seeds) in vegetable dishes; casseroles; pastries; over salads; with cream cheese; or in any dish in place of expensive nuts.

Turmeric. Distinctive, delicate, aromatic flavour. Use *ground* in curries; pickles; stews; kedgeree; seafoods; chicken dishes; rice dishes; sauces; vegetables.

Vanilla. Flavour and scent is sweet and permeating. Use *beans* for infusions for sweets and cakes; as vanilla sugar. Use *essence* in chocolate and coffee sweets and cakes; with fruit; ice cream; custards; milk puddings; sauces; hot chocolate drinks; cakes and candies.

Pomander Balls

Pomander balls make attractive and inexpensive gifts, especially for children to make for Christmas.

These oranges are sometimes called 'clove oranges', which is a good descriptive name. They not only smell nice when hanging in a cupboard or kept in a drawer, but they also are a deterrent to moths.

The oranges shrink as time passes and become as hard as iron, but they do not go bad. They can last for years and years, remaining spicily fragrant.

One of the important ingredients to give a pomander ball its characteristic scent is ground orris root. This is the powdered dried root of the white flowering Florentine iris, *Iris florentina*.

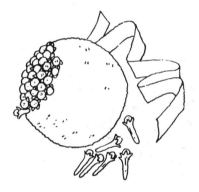

To make a Pomander Ball

Select a thin-skinned, round, ripe orange. Starting from the stalk end, stick it full of cloves – all round and all over the orange.

When covered with cloves, roll it well in one teaspoon of orris powder and one teaspoon of ground cinnamon well mixed together, pressing it in. Then wrap the orange in tissue paper and keep in a dark cupboard for at least two weeks.

Take out the orange and shake off any surplus powder. Either tie a ribbon around it, leaving a loop at the top for hanging, or press a staple into the top of the orange and decorate it with a bow of ribbon. A narrow ribbon can be tied round the orange in two or three places and slipped through the staple leaving a loop above.

Recipe Section

Unless otherwise stated, all herbs used in recipes are dried

Cooking with herbs and spices can become an insidious habit. Once the first voyage of discovery in the kitchen has been navigated successfully, no cook will ever want to be without a well-stocked spice rack.

I have always been enthralled with the flavours of the herb and spice ingredients encountered in different parts of the world which I have visited. And even while at sea, the aroma can be wafted out upon the wind to excite the mind and the palate.

All herbs can be grown in temperate climates and in the Western world can, therefore, be enjoyed in their pristine freshness. But almost all the spices prefer tropical climates, so in England we must be content with the dried varieties.

For their invaluable help to me and for the ingredients of many of the experiments in this book, my grateful thanks go to:

The Royal Horticultural Society's Garden, Wisley, Ripley, Woking, Surrey.

Mr. & Mrs. R. E. Hawkins, The Old Coach House Nurseries, Norton-sub-Hamdon, Somerset.

Sutton & Sons Ltd., The Royal Seed Establishment, Reading, Berkshire.

McCormick Herb and Spice Bureau, 17 Golden Square, London, W.1.

Blue Ribbon Spice Kitchen, 83, Kingsway, London, W.C.2.

Schwartz Spices Ltd., The Spice Centre, 78 White Lion Street, London N.1.

Cooking notes

It is always difficult to convey one's reasons for doing one thing and not doing something else. But so that the reader may understand as many of my reasons as possible, I would like to give a few hints.

1. I have not used composite spices and seasonings because most are hard to find outside large towns.

The only ones which are fairly universal are 'Seasoned Salt' and 'Seasoned Pepper', so these make a few appearances. However, do not let this deter anybody who feels like trying the more exotic mixtures. They are fun, often delicious, and well worth an experiment.

2. Where the word 'fresh' for a herb is mentioned it is much superior to the dried for that particular dish, but half the quantity of the dried variety can always be substituted, unless categorically barred.

3. Wherever butter is mentioned, margarine can be substituted. It is up to the reader to decide whether the additional flavour from butter warrants the extra cost.

5. All oven temperatures and timing is taken from the centre shelf, unless otherwise stated.

A herb box containing, from left to right, tarragon, chives, sage and thyme.
French rice salad (see page 37)

Meal Starters

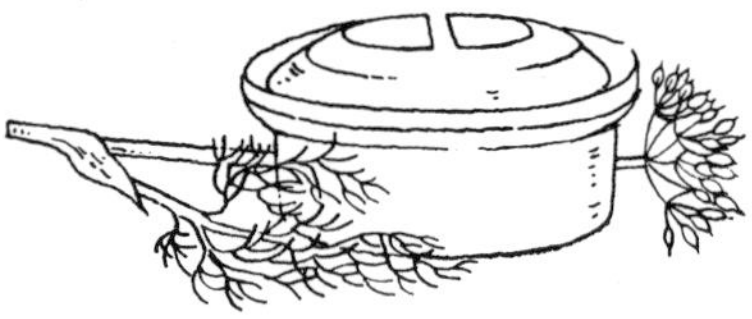

Bilberry soup

Cooking time 5–6 minutes. Serves 6

IMPERIAL	AMERICAN
1 lb. bilberries	1 lb. blueberries
1½ pints water	3¾ cups water
½ teaspoon ground cinnamon	½ teaspoon ground cinnamon
½ teaspoon sweet cicely (optional)	½ teaspoon sweet cicely (optional)
2–3 oz. sugar	4–6 tablespoons sugar
½ tablespoon cornflour	½ tablespoon cornstarch
5 fl. oz. double or single cream	⅔ cup whipping or coffee cream

Wash the bilberries. Bring the water, cinnamon and sweet cicely, if used, to the boil. Add the fruit and 2 oz. (U.S. 4 tablespoons) of the sugar and boil for 3–4 minutes until the fruit is tender. Pulp in a blender/ liquidizer or rub through a sieve.
Mix the cornflour to a smooth paste with a little of the soup, return to the pan, taste and add more sugar if necessary. Bring to the boil, stirring, and boil for a minute or so. Pour into bowls and swirl a tablespoon or more of cream into each if serving hot. Or chill before adding cream, for serving cold.

Chilled tomato soup

No cooking. Serves 4

IMPERIAL	AMERICAN
2 lb. tomatoes	2 lb. tomatoes
½–¾ oz. onion, chopped	approx. 1 tablespoon chopped onion
1 teaspoon fresh tarragon	1 teaspoon fresh tarragon
½ tablespoon tomato purée or ketchup	½ tablespoon tomato paste or catsup
¾ tablespoon sugar	¾ tablespoon sugar
1 teaspoon salt	1 teaspoon salt
pepper	pepper
5 fl. oz. double cream or soured cream	⅔ cup whipping cream or sour cream
chopped chives or parsley	chopped chives or parsley

Wash and quarter the tomatoes. Whisk with the onion and tarragon in a blender/liquidizer until smooth, then rub through a fine sieve. Or rub through a sieve by hand. Stir in the tomato purée thoroughly with the sugar, salt, and pepper to taste.
Chill.
To serve, stir in the cream, pour into soup bowls and garnish with chopped chives or parsley.

Clear bortsch

Cooking time 40–50 minutes. Serves 4–5

IMPERIAL	AMERICAN
1½–2 lb. raw beetroot (the small red kind are best)	1½–2 lb. raw beets
1 quart beef stock (or made with 2 cubes)	5 cups beef stock (or made with 2 bouillon cubes)
¼ teaspoon dill or fennel seeds	¼ teaspoon dill or fennel seeds
salt, pepper	salt, pepper
Smetana or soured cream	Smetana or sour cream
chopped chives or parsley	chopped chives or parsley

Peel and grate the beetroot coarsely. Bring to the boil in the stock with the seeds and salt and pepper to taste (according to the stock used).
Simmer for 40–50 minutes, then strain through a piece of muslin over a strainer.
To serve, bring to boiling point and pour into soup bowls, add a good spoonful of Smetana or soured cream to each bowl and sprinkle with chopped chives or parsley.

Consommé Celestine

This soup is named after Saint Celestine who, in 1294, became Pope Celestine V and was later canonized. The herbed pancakes, which are its feature, can be made a day ahead and kept wrapped. The consommé out of a can is almost as good with a tablespoon or two of dry sherry stirred in.

Cooking time 10–15 minutes. Serves 5–6

IMPERIAL	AMERICAN
1 tablespoon grated Parmesan cheese	1 tablespoon grated Parmesan cheese
½ teaspoon chopped chervil	½ teaspoon chopped chervil
½ teaspoon chopped tarragon	½ teaspoon chopped tarragon
1 teaspoon chopped parsley	1 teaspoon chopped parsley
salt	salt
2 oz. plain flour	½ cup all-purpose flour
1 egg	1 egg
5 fl. oz. milk	⅔ cup milk
1 quart consommé	5 cups consommé

Stir the cheese, herbs and salt into the flour. Mix into a batter with the egg and milk and fry the pancakes as usual. Cut into thin strips. Place as many strips as desired in the soup tureen or bowls, pour over the boiling consommé and serve immediately.

Crème du Barry

Comtesse (known usually as Madame) du Barry was the famous mistress of Louis XV, who awarded the women chef of the Comtesse, the title of 'Cordon Bleu'. Madame du Barry must have been excessively fond of cauliflower, for as a garnish her name denotes cauliflower in some form. The best-known of the dishes named after her is this soup.

Cooking time 30–33 minutes. Serves 5–6

IMPERIAL	AMERICAN
1 lb. cauliflower (without leaves)	1 lb. cauliflower (without leaves)
5–6 oz. potatoes, peeled	$\frac{1}{3}$ lb. potatoes, peeled
1$\frac{1}{4}$ pints water	generous 3 cups water
salt, pepper	salt, pepper
$\frac{1}{4}$ teaspoon ground nutmeg	$\frac{1}{4}$ teaspoon ground nutmeg
13 fl. oz. milk	approx. 1$\frac{1}{2}$ cups milk
$\frac{1}{2}$ oz. butter	1 tablespoon butter

Cut the cauliflower and potatoes into rough pieces and bring to the boil in the water, with 2 teaspoons salt. Simmer, covered, for 30 minutes, then blend in a liquidizer or rub through a sieve. Add the nutmeg and milk, adjust seasoning and boil for 2–3 minutes. Remove from the heat and stir in the butter gradually. Serve with fried croûtons of bread.

Gazpacho Andaluz

This famous Spanish soup can be made in dozens of different ways. The version I give here is the one I learned in Andaluzia; I thought it was one of the nicest I had tasted.

No cooking. Serves 6

IMPERIAL	AMERICAN
2 oz. crustless white bread	2 slices crustless white bread
1$\frac{1}{2}$ pints water	3$\frac{3}{4}$ cups water
1$\frac{1}{2}$ lb. tomatoes, skinned	1$\frac{1}{2}$ lb. tomatoes, skinned
6 oz. (1 medium) cucumber	1 medium cucumber (6 oz.)
2$\frac{1}{2}$–3 oz. green pepper flesh	flesh 1 sweet green pepper
5 oz. onion, peeled	1 medium onion, peeled
1 large or 2 small cloves garlic, chopped and crushed	1 large or 2 small cloves garlic, chopped and crushed
$\frac{1}{2}$ teaspoon ground cumin	$\frac{1}{2}$ teaspoon ground cumin
3 tablespoons wine vinegar	scant $\frac{1}{4}$ cup wine vinegar
1 teaspoon salt	1 teaspoon salt

Soak the roughly crumbled bread in $\frac{1}{2}$ pint (U.S. 1$\frac{1}{4}$ cups) of the water until soft, then beat it up. Stir in the roughly chopped vegetables and the rest of the ingredients and leave to soak for at least 3–4 hours, or overnight.
Blend everything in a liquidizer and then rub through a fine sieve. Chill thoroughly.
Hand the following items separately, all finely cubed: flesh 1 green pepper; 8 oz. tomatoes, skinned and seeded; 2–3 oz. cucumber, unpeeled; 2 slices bread from a sliced sandwich loaf, crusts removed.

French rice salad

(illustrated in colour on page 34)

Serve this salad in sundae glasses as a first course. For a main course salad, increase the quantities by about a third and pile into a large bowl.

Cooking time 15–18 minutes. Serves 4–5

IMPERIAL	AMERICAN
4 oz. long grain rice	generous $\frac{1}{2}$ cup long grain rice
salt, pepper	salt, pepper
2 oz. blue cheese	$\frac{1}{2}$ cup crumbled blue cheese
2 teaspoons lemon juice	2 teaspoons lemon juice
5 fl. oz. soured cream	$\frac{2}{3}$ cup sour cream
2 sticks (3 oz.) celery	2 stalks celery
10–12 (2 oz.) radishes (optional)	10–12 radishes (optional)
2-inch piece (2 oz.) cucumber	2-inch piece cucumber
8–10 oz. tomatoes	about $\frac{1}{2}$ lb. tomatoes
1$\frac{1}{2}$ teaspoons fresh dill, chopped (or $\frac{3}{4}$ teaspoon dried dill weed)	1$\frac{1}{2}$ teaspoons fresh dill, chopped (or $\frac{3}{4}$ teaspoon dried dill weed)
2 teaspoons fresh marjoram, chopped (or 1$\frac{1}{4}$ teaspoons dried)	2 teaspoons fresh marjoram, chopped (or 1$\frac{1}{4}$ teaspoons dried)
$\frac{3}{4}$–1 tablespoon chopped chives	$\frac{3}{4}$–1 tablespoon chopped chives

Drop the rice into boiling, salted water and boil for 15–18 minutes, until the rice is tender but still retains a slight 'bite' in the centre.
Drain well. Or cook by the absorption method. Put rice, $\frac{1}{2}$ pint (U.S. 1$\frac{1}{4}$ cups) water and $\frac{1}{2}$ teaspoon salt into a saucepan. Bring to the boil and stir, cover and simmer for 15–18 minutes or until all the liquid has been absorbed.
Crumble the cheese roughly and mix with the lemon juice and two-thirds of the soured cream. Wash and slice the celery and radishes, if used, finely and cut the unpeeled cucumber into $\frac{1}{4}$–$\frac{1}{2}$-inch cubes. Cut the tomatoes into wedges, keep some aside for garnish and chop the rest. Mix the vegetables and herbs together and pile into sundae glasses.
Put a spoonful of the remaining soured cream on top of each. Garnish with the reserved tomato wedges and a sprig of dill if possible.

Potato chervil soup

(illustrated in colour on page 38)

A particularly delicious soup to serve as a supper dish or as a 'warmer-upper' after an evening's outing. The time and trouble can be cut considerably by using an instant potato powder, in place of the raw potato.
For this method, increase the stock to 2 pints (U.S. 5 cups) and simmer for 10–15 minutes only, then sprinkle the contents of a large (5-oz.) packet of instant potato on to the boiling liquid and stir thoroughly. Finish off as below.
The chervil must not be cooked or it will loose much of its flavour, so add it only after the soup has been removed from the heat.

Cooking time 55–60 minutes *or shorter method* 20–25 minutes. *Serves 4–5*

IMPERIAL	AMERICAN
1 lb. potatoes, after peeling	1 lb. potatoes, after peeling
4 oz. onion, peeled	1 small onion, peeled
1 oz. butter	2 tablespoons butter
1½ pints white stock	3¾ cups white stock
1 small bay leaf	1 small bay leaf
⅛ teaspoon ground mace	⅛ teaspoon ground mace
5 fl. oz. single cream or milk	⅔ cup coffee cream or milk
salt, pepper	salt, pepper
5–6 tablespoons chopped chervil	6–7 tablespoons chopped chervil

Slice the potato and onion. Melt the butter and sweat the vegetables gently with the pan covered, stirring occasionally, for 8–10 minutes. Pour in the stock. Add the bay leaf and mace and simmer, covered, for 45–50 minutes.
Remove the bay leaf and put the soup through a liquidizer or rub through a sieve. Stir in the cream or milk and season to taste with salt and pepper. Reheat, then remove from the heat and stir in the chervil. Serve with fried croûtons, if liked.

Sinhalese soup

The lovely Cyd Charisse has the graceful svelte lines of a former ballerina, yet enjoys the fattening foods without detriment to her figure. Particularly fond is she of soups – hot and cold. And this adaptation of Mulligatawny can be served hot or cold.

Cooking time 40 minutes. *Serves 4*

IMPERIAL	AMERICAN
2–3 oz. onion	½ onion
1 clove garlic	1 clove garlic
6 oz. tomatoes	⅓ lb. tomatoes
1 medium cooking apple	1 medium baking apple
½ oz. butter	1 tablespoon butter
1 tablespoon oil	1 tablespoon oil
½ tablespoon curry powder	½ tablespoon curry powder
½ teaspoon ground cumin	½ teaspoon ground cumin
¼ teaspoon ground turmeric	¼ teaspoon ground turmeric
½ teaspoon salt	½ teaspoon salt
1 oz. flour	¼ cup all-purpose flour
1 quart chicken stock, or made from 2 stock cubes	5 cups chicken stock, or made from 2 bouillon cubes
½ tablespoon lemon juice	½ tablespoon lemon juice

Slice the onion finely, chop and crush the garlic, skin and chop the tomatoes and chop half the unpeeled apple.
In a thick-bottomed saucepan, gently fry the onion and garlic in the butter and oil until amber coloured. Add the tomato, chopped apple, spices and salt, cover and allow to sweat for about 5 minutes, stirring occasionally.
Make the flour into a paste with a little of the stock, add to the pan with the rest of the stock and boil gently, uncovered, for 30 minutes. Blend in a liquidizer or rub through a sieve. Stir in the lemon juice, adjust seasoning and add the rest of the apple, peeled and grated on a medium grater.

Norwegian sea-fruit cocktail

No cooking. Serves 4

IMPERIAL	AMERICAN
4–6 oz. fresh shelled or frozen prawns	¼–⅓ lb. fresh peeled or frozen prawns
½ canteloup or honeydew melon	½ canteloup or honeydew melon
1½ tablespoons cream	2 tablespoons cream
½–¾ teaspoon curry powder	½–¾ teaspoon curry powder
¼ teaspoon paprika pepper	¼ teaspoon paprika pepper
4 tablespoons mayonnaise	5 tablespoons mayonnaise
salt	salt
sprigs of dill or mint leaves	sprigs of dill or mint leaves

If the prawns are frozen, allow them to thaw out thoroughly. Reserve four good ones for garnish. Cut the flesh of the melon into balls with a ball cutter, or into small cubes, and reserve four also.
Beat the cream, curry powder and paprika into the mayonnaise and season with salt to taste.
Turn the prawns and melon into four shallow sundae glasses and spoon over the sauce. Garnish with the reserved prawns and melon and a sprig of dill, or one or two mint leaves.

Potato chervil soup and Dubonnet terrine
(see pages 39 and 48)

Giblet soup

An excellent way to finish off the poultry after a party.

Cooking time 1½–2 hours. *Serves* 5

IMPERIAL	AMERICAN
giblets from 2 chickens or ducks	giblets from 2 chickens or ducks
2½ pints bird stock	6¼ cups bird stock
2 oz. onion, peeled	½ onion, peeled
2 oz. carrot, peeled	2 small carrots, peeled
bouquet garni or	bouquet garni or
1 teaspoon mixed herbs	1 teaspoon mixed herbs
salt, pepper	salt, pepper
1¼ oz. flour	5 tablespoons all-purpose flour
1–2 tablespoons port (optional)	1–3 tablespoons port (optional)
chopped parsley	chopped parsley

Wash the giblets thoroughly, remove all the fat and cut the meat into pieces. Turn into a pan with the necks and the stock. Bring to the boil, skim well, then add the roughly chopped onion and carrot, herbs, and salt and pepper to taste. Simmer, covered, for 1½–2 hours until the giblets are quite tender.
Cut all the meat off the necks and then blend in a liquidizer or rub through a sieve.
Make the flour into a paste with a little of the soup and stir into the rest. Bring to the boil, stirring, and boil for 3–4 minutes. Stir in the port, if used, just before serving and sprinkle with chopped parsley.

Green pepper summer cream

Cooking time 45–50 minutes. *Serves* 4

IMPERIAL	AMERICAN
1 large (8–10 oz.) or two smaller green peppers	1 large or 2 smaller sweet green peppers
1¼ pints chicken stock	generous 3 cups chicken stock
1 teaspoon mixed herbs	1 teaspoon mixed herbs
¼ oz. (½ tablespoon) cornflour	½ tablespoon cornstarch
½ tablespoon cold water	½ tablespoon cold water
5 fl. oz. soured cream or yogurt	⅔ cup sour cream or yogurt
chopped parsley	chopped parsley

Wash the peppers, remove the stalks and seeds and chop the flesh roughly. Bring to the boil with the stock and herbs and boil, covered, for 40–45 minutes. Turn into a liquidizer and blend until smooth, then pour through a sieve into a saucepan. Or rub through a sieve by hand. Make the cornflour into a paste with the water, stir into the soup, bring to the boil stirring and boil for 2–3 minutes. When cool, stir in the soured cream, season if necessary and chill.
Serve garnished with chopped parsley.

Sopa Triton

I was taught this delicious soup by Chef Alfredo Diz of the Triton Hotel in Torremolinos on Spain's Costa del Sol.

Cooking time 20–25 minutes. *Serves* 4

IMPERIAL	AMERICAN
1½ oz. leek, very finely chopped	1 small leek, very finely chopped
1 oz. carrot, very finely chopped	1 small carrot, very finely chopped
1½ tablespoons fresh tarragon (or ¾ tablespoon dried)	2 tablespoons fresh tarragon (or ¾ tablespoon dried)
1 oz. butter	2 tablespoons butter
½ pint chicken stock	1¼ cups chicken stock
8–9 oz. potato, peeled	generous ½ lb. potatoes, peeled
1 egg yolk	1 egg yolk
½ pint single cream	1¼ cups coffee cream
salt, pepper	salt, pepper

Fry the leek, carrot and tarragon in the butter for 5–7 minutes, until they are fairly soft.
Remove from heat and stir in the stock.
Boil the potato and mash well (better still rub through a sieve). Beat in the egg yolk thoroughly. Stir in the cream and then the vegetables.
Season to taste.
Chill well and stir before serving.

Mushrooms à la grecque

This dish can be served on its own as a first course, or as one of several for an hors d'oeuvre for 6 to 8 people.

Cooking time 9–11 minutes. *Serves* 4

IMPERIAL	AMERICAN
8 oz. small button mushrooms	2 cups small button mushrooms
1 (8 oz.) can tomatoes	1 (8 oz.) can tomatoes
2–3 oz. onion, peeled	½ onion, peeled
5 fl. oz. olive oil	⅔ cup olive oil
2 twigs thyme	2 twigs thyme
½ bay leaf	½ bay leaf
6 peppercorns, lightly crushed	6 peppercorns, lightly crushed
½ teaspoon salt	½ teaspoon salt

Wash and dry the mushrooms and cut any larger ones in halves. Rub the tomatoes through a sieve. Slice the onion lengthways, fairly thinly. Heat the oil in a saucepan, turn everything into it, cover and simmer until tender, about 10 minutes.
Serve cold.

Fish

Baked stuffed pike, bass, cod, haddock (jewfish)

Any of these fishes are good when stuffed and baked in this manner.

Cooking time 40–45 minutes.
Serves 4
Oven temperature 350° F., 180° C., Gas Mark 4

IMPERIAL	AMERICAN
2½–3 lb. fish	2½–3 lb. fish
3 oz. onion, very finely chopped	¾ cup very finely chopped onion
¾ tablespoon chopped capers	¾ tablespoon chopped capers
½ teaspoon chopped lemon (or common) thyme	½ teaspoon chopped lemon (or common) thyme
1 teaspoon dill weed	1 teaspoon dill weed
1 teaspoon salt	1 teaspoon salt
good grinding black pepper	freshly cracked black pepper
2 oz. soft breadcrumbs	1 cup soft bread crumbs
3 oz. butter, melted	6 tablespoons melted butter
1 small egg, beaten	1 small egg, beaten
dried breadcrumbs	fine dried bread crumbs
1½ oz. butter	3 tablespoons butter
1½ tablespoons oil	2 tablespoons oil

Scrub the fish well to remove all the scales. Cut off gills and fins and trim the tail, but leave the head intact. Slit down the belly of the fish from head to tail and carefully cut out the backbone.
Make the stuffing. Mix the onion, capers, herbs and seasoning with the breadcrumbs, then stir in the melted butter. Stuff the fish with the mixture and sew up with a darning needle and thread. Brush all over with beaten egg, sprinkle with salt and pat on a coating of dried breadcrumbs. Melt the rest of the butter and the oil in a baking tin, lay in the fish and baste well. Bake in a moderate oven, basting occasionally, for 40–45 minutes.
Turn over once carefully.
Serve with Tartare sauce, see page 62, or a piquant sauce, if liked.

Cod's roe pie

Cooking time 30–35 minutes. *Serves* 4–5
Oven temperature 400° F., 200° C., Gas Mark 6

IMPERIAL	AMERICAN
1 lb. cod's roe, cooked	1 lb. cod's roe, cooked
2 oz. onion, finely chopped	½ cup finely chopped onion
1½ oz. butter or margarine	3 tablespoons butter or margarine
1 oz. flour	¼ cup all-purpose flour
½ pint milk	1¼ cups milk
½ teaspoon mixed herbs	½ teaspoon mixed herbs
½ teaspoon salt	½ teaspoon salt
good shake pepper	dash pepper
4–5 frankfurters, sliced thinly	4–5 frankfurters, sliced thinly
dried breadcrumbs	fine dry bread crumbs

Pull off all the skin from the roe (or buy already processed) and mash flesh with a fork.
Fry the onion in the butter, until a light golden brown. Blend in the flour, add the milk gradually, stirring, and bring to the boil. Mix with the herbs and seasonings into the roe.
Place half the mixture in a deep heatproof dish, dot all over with the sliced frankfurters, and cover with the rest of the roe. Sprinkle with the dried breadcrumbs, dot with flakes of butter and bake in a moderately hot oven for 20–25 minutes until nicely browned.

Grilled herring with fennel

Cooking time 8–10 minutes. *Serves* 4

IMPERIAL	AMERICAN
4 (6–8 oz.) herrings	4 (6–8 oz.) herrings
2 tablespoons chopped fresh fennel	3 tablespoons chopped fresh fennel
½ tablespoon salt	½ tablespoon salt
1 oz. butter	2 tablespoons butter
1 teaspoon lemon juice	1 teaspoon lemon juice

Wash and scrub the fish well to remove all scales. Cut off the heads and trim the tails. Cut three narrow slits on the slant across each side. Mix the fennel and salt together and insert into the cuts and in the body cavity.
Melt the butter and lemon juice in a grill pan. Lay the fish in it and at once turn over so that all the fish is coated. Grill under a hot grill for 4–5 minutes each side, basting once.

VARIATION: When fresh fennel is not available, use ¾ tablespoon dried fennel or dill seeds instead.

Roulade de sole
(see page 44)

Cod Portugaise
(see opposite)

Court bouillon

Fish should never be 'boiled', hence the term 'poached'. In other words, the liquid should not be allowed to be on a fast boil when the fish is lowered into it, and thereafter bubbles should hardly break the surface.

To poach fish in court bouillon, prior to serving with a sauce, gives a far superior flavour than when cooked in plain salted water.

If a fish kettle with its own strainer is not used, wrap the fish in muslin so that it can be manoeuvred easily without fear of breaking.

Fish suitable for poaching in court bouillon, whole or in cutlets or fillets, are: bass, cod, conger eel, haddock, fresh, (*jewfish*), hake, halibut, herring (*mullet*), grey mullet, John Dory, mackerel, pike, skate (*wings*), sole (*flounder*), and turbot.

IMPERIAL	AMERICAN
1 quart water	5 cups water
any fish trimmings (tail, bones, skin, etc.)	any fish trimmings (tail, bones, skin, etc.)
1 carrot	1 carrot
1 medium onion	1 medium onion
½ tablespoon salt	½ tablespoon salt
4–5 peppercorns, crushed	4–5 peppercorns, crushed
bouquet garni	bouquet garni
1 bay leaf	1 bay leaf
1 oz. celery or ½ teaspoon celery seeds	1 stalk celery or ½ teaspoon celery seeds
1 tablespoon vinegar	1 tablespoon vinegar
2 tablespoons white wine or vinegar	3 tablespoons white wine or vinegar

Bring everything to the boil in a covered pan and boil for 30 minutes to 1 hour. Strain before use. This stock will keep in a refrigerator for several days.

Grilled mackerel with mustard dill sauce

Cooking time 8–10 minutes. Serve 4

IMPERIAL	AMERICAN
4 (about 8 oz. each) mackerel	4 (about ½ lb. each) mackerel
salt	salt
2 oz. butter	¼ cup butter
1 teaspoon lemon juice	1 teaspoon lemon juice
½ tablespoon mustard powder	½ tablespoon mustard powder
1 teaspoon anchovy essence	1 teaspoon anchovy extract
½ tablespoon vinegar	½ tablespoon vinegar
¾ oz. flour	3 tablespoons all-purpose flour
8 fl. oz. milk	about 1 cup milk
bare ½ teaspoon chopped dill weed	scant ½ teaspoon chopped dill weed

Wash thoroughly and clean the mackerel, remove the heads and trim the tails. Cut three narrow slits on the slant across each side. Sprinkle with salt.
Melt half the butter with the lemon juice in a grill pan. Lay the fish in it and at once turn over so that all the fish is coated. Grill under a hot grill for 4 to 5 minutes each side, basting once.
Meanwhile make the sauce. Stir the mustard powder into a paste with the anchovy essence and vinegar. In a small saucepan, melt the rest of the butter, blend in the flour, add the milk and stir with a wire whisk until it boils. Boil for a minute or two, then stir in the mustard mixture, dill weed and salt to taste. Bring again to the boil for serving.

VARIATION: The mackerel may be slit open and the bones removed before grilling. Grill flat, allowing a minute or two less each side. They may also be filleted before grilling.

Cod Portugaise

(illustrated in colour on page 42)

Cooking time 30–35 minutes. Serves 4
Oven temperature 350° F., 180° C., Gas Mark 4

IMPERIAL	AMERICAN
1 lb. tomatoes	1 lb. tomatoes
4 (8 oz.) cod cutlets	4 (½ lb.) cod cutlets
butter	butter
salt, pepper	salt, pepper
2–3 oz. onion, finely chopped	½–¾ cup finely chopped onion
1 clove garlic, chopped and crushed (optional)	1 clove garlic, chopped and crushed (optional)
1 teaspoon chopped parsley	1 teaspoon chopped parsley
¼ teaspoon thyme	¼ teaspoon thyme
¼ teaspoon basil	¼ teaspoon basil
tarragon or wine vinegar	tarragon or wine vinegar
water	water
1 teaspoon sugar	1 teaspoon sugar

Skin and chop the tomatoes. Wash, trim and tie the cod cutlets into a neat shape. Place them in a buttered, shallow heatproof dish and sprinkle with salt and pepper, the tomato, onion, garlic and herbs. Pour in equal quantities of vinegar and water to come halfway up the cutlets. Cover the dish with foil or greaseproof paper and bake in a moderate oven for 30–35 minutes. Pour the liquid from the dish into a small saucepan. Stir in the sugar and leaving the pan uncovered, boil rapidly to reduce by half. Garnish the dish around the fish with vegetables, serving the sauce separately.

Roulade de sole

(illustrated in colour on page 42)

Cooking time 30–35 minutes. *Serves* 4
Oven temperature 375° F., 190° C., Gas Mark 5

IMPERIAL	AMERICAN
2 (1½–2 lb.) soles	2 (1½–2 lb.) flounder
1 small banana	1 small banana
1 (2 oz. flesh) small cooking apple	1 small baking apple
¼ teaspoon dill weed	¼ teaspoon dill weed
½ teaspoon chopped chives	½ teaspoon chopped chives
1 oz. soft breadcrumbs	½ cup soft bread crumbs
salt, pepper	salt, pepper
1 egg	1 egg
1 medium onion	1 medium onion
½ pint water	1¼ cups water
2 tablespoons Grand Marnier	3 tablespoons Grand Marnier
2 oz. button mushrooms (optional)	½ cup button mushrooms (optional)
sprigs parsley	sprigs parsley

Ask the fishmonger to skin and fillet the sole and to give you the skin and bones.

Chop the peeled banana and apple into small cubes and mix with the dill weed, chives and breadcrumbs. Season to taste with salt and pepper and bind with beaten egg. Divide into 8 portions.

Lay the fillets, skinned side down on a board, spread a portion of stuffing along each and roll up, starting from the wide end. Secure with thread. Place the skin and bones in a heatproof dish with the roughly sliced onion. Stand the rolls of fish on top and pour in the water and Grand Marnier. Cover with greaseproof paper and bake in a moderate oven for 25 minutes. Meanwhile, if used, wipe the mushrooms with a damp cloth, slice fairly thickly and sauté in a little butter and milk in a covered pan, for 2–3 minutes. Drain.

Remove the fish to a hot serving dish and cut off the thread. Pour over the sauce and arrange the mushroom slices on top of each roll, garnishing with sprigs of parsley.

Sauce

IMPERIAL	AMERICAN
liquor from fish	liquor from fish
cream or milk	cream or milk
1½ oz. butter	3 tablespoons butter
1½ oz. flour	6 tablespoons all-purpose flour
3 tablespoons Grand Marnier	4 tablespoons Grand Marnier
salt, pepper	salt, pepper

Strain the liquor from the fish and make up to ¾ pint (U.S. 2 cups) with cream or milk. Melt the butter in a small saucepan, blend in the flour and add the liquid. Bring to the boil, stirring with a wire whisk. Boil for 2–3 minutes and remove from the heat. Add the Grand Marnier and season to taste with salt and pepper.

Fish salad

Don't try this salad without the coriander!

Cooking time 12–16 minutes. *Serves* 4

IMPERIAL	AMERICAN
1½ lb. fillet of white fish (cod, haddock, etc.)	1½ lb. fillet of white fish (cod, haddock, etc.)
6–8 spring onions, very finely chopped	6–8 scallions, very finely chopped
½ tablespoon ground coriander	½ tablespoon ground coriander
salt, pepper	salt, pepper
1 tablespoon tarragon vinegar	1 tablespoon tarragon vinegar
2–3 tablespoons wine vinegar	3–4 tablespoons wine vinegar

Wash the fish and drop it into gently boiling, salted water. Simmer until cooked, about 12–16 minutes, depending upon the thickness of the fillet. Drain, remove skin and bones and flake the flesh.

Place a layer of fish in a decorative bowl, sprinkle with onion, coriander, salt and pepper. Repeat layers. Pour over the vinegars, mixed, and leave for several hours before serving, or until the following day in a refrigerator.

Tulya

Cooking time 35–40 minutes. *Serves* 4

IMPERIAL	AMERICAN
1 lb. fillet cod, haddock, or any white fish	1 lb. fillet cod, haddock, or any white fish
juice ½ small lemon	juice ½ small lemon
salt	salt
8 oz. potatoes	½ lb. potatoes
2 oz. rashers streaky bacon	3 slices bacon
1 tablespoon oil	1 tablespoon oil
4 oz. onion, sliced	1 medium onion, sliced
1 tablespoon tomato purée	1 tablespoon tomato paste
½ pint water	1¼ cups water
⅛ teaspoon cayenne pepper	⅛ teaspoon cayenne pepper
¼ teaspoon sugar	¼ teaspoon sugar
½ teaspoon basil	½ teaspoon basil

Cut the flesh off the skin of the fish and cut in large cubes, sprinkle with the lemon juice and salt to taste. Peel and cut the potatoes into rough ½-inch cubes.

Cut the bacon into inch-sized pieces and fry in the oil with the onion over moderate heat, until the onion is soft and just beginning to colour. Pour in the tomato purée mixed with the water, cayenne and sugar. Add the potato and basil, cover the pan and simmer for 20 minutes stirring occasionally, then add the fish and continue cooking for 10–15 minutes without stirring.

Prawn curry

Without the fresh spices and coconut milk with which this curry is made in India, it can be but a poor substitute here, but it is still very good.

Fresh coconuts can be bought at certain times, and the grated flesh from one of these will give a far richer and fresher coconut milk than that made from desiccated coconut.

Cooking time 18–20 minutes. Serves 4

IMPERIAL	AMERICAN
¾ pint boiling water	2 cups boiling water
5 oz. desiccated coconut	1⅔ cups shredded coconut
2 tablespoons ground coriander	3 tablespoons ground coriander
1 tablespoon ground cumin (jeera)	1 tablespoon ground cumin (jeera)
½ tablespoon ground turmeric	½ tablespoon ground turmeric
1½ teaspoons ground ginger	1½ teaspoons ground ginger
¾ teaspoon chilli powder (or a little less cayenne pepper)	¾ teaspoon chilli powder (or a little less cayenne pepper)
1 teaspoon salt	1 teaspoon salt
2 tablespoons tamarind juice or vinegar	3 tablespoons tamarind juice or vinegar
6 oz. onion, sliced finely	1 large onion, sliced finely
2 large cloves garlic, crushed	2 large cloves garlic, crushed
3 tablespoons oil	4 tablespoons oil
1 lb. shelled, fresh or frozen prawns	1 lb. peeled, fresh or frozen prawns

Pour the boiling water over the coconut and, when cool enough to handle, squeeze out as much milk as possible through a sieve. Make a paste of the spices and salt, with the tamarind juice or vinegar.
In a heatproof casserole or frying pan, fry the onion and garlic in the oil until amber coloured. Stir in the curry paste and continue frying, stirring continuously, for 3–4 minutes. Pour in the coconut milk and simmer, uncovered, for 10 minutes. Add the prawns, adjust seasoning and heat through.
Serve with boiled rice (allow 12 oz. (U.S. 1¾ cups) long grain rice for 4), poppadums (to cook see page 48), Bombay duck (dried fish) and sambals (side dishes).

Paella à la Valenciana

Paella is made with different ingredients combined with the rice in the various regions of Spain. The most colourful, and therefore the best known, is the combination which comes from Valenciana.

A heavy copper, omelette-shaped pan with two handles called a 'sarten' is the traditional dish in which paella is cooked and served. If no sarten or frying pan large enough to take all the ingredients is available (it is not worth making a small quantity), the frying can be done in a frying pan and then the whole lot transferred to a casserole.
Calamari (cuttle-fish) or squid are also usually included in this dish, cut into rounds and fried with the onion.

Cooking time 28–30 minutes. Serves 8–9

IMPERIAL	AMERICAN
14–16 mussels	14–16 mussels
2–2½ lb. chicken	2–2½ lb. chicken
1 pork fillet	1 pork tenderloin
1 (4 oz.) can pimentos	1 (4 oz.) can pimientos
4–5 tablespoons olive oil	5–6 tablespoons olive oil
4–5 oz. onion, finely chopped	1–1¼ cups finely chopped onion
1 large clove garlic, crushed	1 large clove garlic, crushed
2 small tomatoes, skinned and chopped	2 small tomatoes, skinned and chopped
12 oz. long grain rice	approx. 1¾ cups long grain rice
1½ pints hot water	3¾ cups hot water
few shreds saffron	few shreds saffron
1 bay leaf	1 bay leaf
½ tablespoon salt	½ tablespoon salt
good milling black pepper	freshly cracked black pepper
8 oz. French beans, cut in halves	½ lb. green beans, cut in halves
2–3 oz. shelled, fresh or frozen prawns	approx. ½ cup peeled, fresh or frozen prawns
1 crawfish or lobster, cooked	1 crawfish or lobster, cooked

Soak the mussels in salted water, then scrub well and cut off the 'beard'. Place in a thick bottomed pan over high heat, cover tightly, and as soon as they open (in 2–3 minutes) remove them and discard the empty shells. Throw away any which do not open. Cut the chicken into small joints, the pork fillet into small pieces, and the pimentos into ¼–½-inch pieces.
Gently fry the chicken and pork in the oil until they are a light golden colour, add the onion and garlic and continue frying for 3–4 minutes. Stir in the tomatoes and rice, add a little more oil if necessary, and fry for a further 3–4 minutes. Pour in the hot water with the saffron infused in it. Stir in the bay leaf, broken in half, with the salt, pepper, beans, pimiento and the prawns and allow to boil for about 20 minutes, or until the rice has absorbed all the liquid.
Serve with the chicken joints and mussels arranged on top and the pieces of crawfish or lobster sticking up from the rice.

Shrimp à la créole

After a glorious swim in a Boston swimming pool, my friend's white-haired negro butler served this dish under the trees. Nothing could have tasted better. It is almost as good indoors as out.

Cooking time 35–40 minutes. Serves 4

IMPERIAL	AMERICAN
1 (5–6 oz.) green pepper	1 sweet green pepper
2 oz. canned pimentos	2 oz. canned pimientos
6 oz. onion, coarsely chopped	1½ cups coarsely chopped onion
5–6 oz. celery, sliced finely	⅓ lb. celery, sliced finely
2 oz. bacon fat or lard	¼ cup bacon drippings or lard
1½ lb. canned tomatoes	1½ lb. canned tomatoes
3 tablespoons tomato purée	4 tablespoons tomato paste
1 large clove garlic, chopped finely	1 large clove garlic, chopped finely
1 teaspoon paprika pepper	1 teaspoon paprika pepper
¼ teaspoon cayenne pepper	¼ teaspoon cayenne pepper
1 bay leaf	1 bay leaf
1 teaspoon salt	1 teaspoon salt
1½ teaspoons sugar	1½ teaspoons sugar
12 oz. fresh, shelled or frozen prawns or shrimps	¾ lb. fresh, peeled or frozen prawns or shrimp

Remove the stalk and seeds from the green pepper and chop the flesh into ¼–½-inch pieces. Chop the pimientos to about the same size.

Fry the green pepper, onion and celery in the fat until lightly coloured. Add the chopped tomatoes with their liquid and the rest of the ingredients, except the pimientos and prawns. Cover the pan and simmer gently for 25–30 minutes until the vegetables are tender. Add the prawns and pimiento and continue cooking for 5–7 minutes.

Serve with boiled rice.

Kedgeree

Although Kedgeree is known as a breakfast dish, it is also delicious for supper and for parties. For these occasions, thinly sliced onion fried until brown and then dried, is particularly good scattered over the top. These dried onions can now be bought in packets, which saves a lot of trouble.

The rice is also much more attractive looking if it is coloured in the Indian way, with turmeric or saffron.

Cooking time 16–20 minutes. Serves 4

IMPERIAL	AMERICAN
1 lb. smoked haddock, cooked (1½–1¾ lb. on the bone, then cooked in milk and water)	1 lb. smoked haddock, cooked (1½–1¾ lb. on the bone, then cooked in milk and water)
2–3 hard-boiled eggs	2–3 hard-cooked eggs
8 oz. long grain rice	generous 1 cup long grain rice
3–4 oz. onion, chopped finely	¾–1 cup finely chopped onion
4 oz. butter	½ cup butter
¾ teaspoon turmeric	¾ teaspoon turmeric
1 bay leaf	1 bay leaf
salt, pepper	salt, pepper
chopped parsley	chopped parsley

Remove bones and skin from the haddock and flake the flesh roughly. Slice one egg and keep aside the good slices for decoration. Chop the rest of the eggs. Drop the rice into boiling, salted water and boil until just tender, 12–14 minutes. Drain well.

Fry the onion gently in the butter for 3–4 minutes until soft but not coloured, add the turmeric and bay leaf and continue frying for a minute. Stir in the fish, then the rice and egg and heat through over a gentle heat without stirring too much. Season with salt and pepper and turn out on to a hot dish.

Decorate with the reserved slices of hard-boiled egg, chopped parsley and dried fried onion if liked.

NOTE: The butter may be decreased and 1–2 tablespoons cream substituted and mixed in just before serving. This is especially good when serving as a breakfast dish.

Stuffed herrings

Cooking time 25–30 minutes. Serves 4
Oven temperature 375° F., 190° C., Gas Mark 5

IMPERIAL	AMERICAN
4 large or 8 small herrings	4 large or 8 small herring
salt, pepper	salt, pepper
2 oz. soft breadcrumbs	1 cup fresh soft bread crumbs
1 oz. shredded suet	3 tablespoons shredded suet
1 oz. onion, finely chopped	¼ cup finely chopped onion
½ teaspoon mixed herbs	½ teaspoon mixed herbs
1 teaspoon chopped parsley	1 teaspoon chopped parsley
½–¾ oz. walnuts, chopped	scant ¼ cup chopped walnuts
½ teaspoon salt	½ teaspoon salt
milled black pepper	freshly cracked black pepper
1 egg	1 egg
butter	butter

Scrub the herrings well to remove all the scales. Cut off the heads and tails. Split the fish down the belly from head to tail. Clean and pull out backbones

carefully, and as many of the small bones as possible. Lay the fish flat, flesh upwards and season.
To make the stuffing. Mix rest of dry ingredients together and bind lightly with the beaten egg. Spread evenly over the fish, roll up and tie with string. Pack the rolls into a heatproof dish, dot with flakes of butter and bake in a moderate oven for 25–30 minutes.
Serve with Mustard Dill Sauce (see page 43), if liked.

Gracie Fields' fish stew

The inimitable Gracie Fields, the one and only 'Lancashire Lass', told me, 'No, no, I have never *thought* of dieting. I love food. Food – all of it.' Despite her restaurant in Capri, she loves the 'beautiful fish in England' and makes a bee-line for it whenever she visits her home country.
This is one of her special recipes which incorporates a cunning tang of ginger.

Cooking time 17–22 minutes. *Serves* 4

IMPERIAL	AMERICAN
2 lb. halibut, turbot, hake, or 4 mackerel	2 lb. halibut, hake, or 4 mackerel
4 oz. onion, sliced finely	1 medium onion sliced finely
1 teaspoon salt	1 teaspoon salt
⅛ teaspoon white pepper	⅛ teaspoon white pepper
½ tablespoon cornflour	½ tablespoon cornstarch
½ teaspoon ground ginger	½ teaspoon ground ginger
4 fl. oz. lemon juice (about 3 lemons)	½ cup lemon juice
2 eggs, beaten	2 eggs, beaten

Cut the fish into serving portions. Turn the onion into a large deep frying pan and cover with ½–¾ inch water. Stir in salt and pepper, cover the pan, bring to the boil and boil for 3–4 minutes. Place the fish flat in the pan (the water should come halfway up the fish) and simmer, covered, for 10–15 minutes or until the fish is cooked. Remove the fish to a hot dish and, with a straining spoon, scatter the onions over the fish.
Make the cornflour and ginger into a paste with the lemon juice. Whisk in the beaten eggs, then ½ pint (U.S. 1¼ cups) of the strained fish liquor. Bring to the boil in a small saucepan, stirring all the time, and simmer for 2–3 minutes; adjust seasoning and pour over the fish.

Meat

Ceylon beef curry
(illustrated in colour on page 49)

The national dish in Ceylon, as in India, is a curry, but more often than not their curries include tomatoes which grow in many parts of the island, and fresh coconut milk. If a fresh coconut is not available, make the milk from desiccated coconut.

Cooking time 1¼–1¾ hours. *Serves* 4

IMPERIAL	AMERICAN
1½ lb. stewing steak	1½ lb. beef stew meat
5 fl. oz. boiling water	⅔ cup boiling water
5 oz. desiccated coconut	1⅔ cups shredded coconut
8–10 oz. onion, chopped finely	2–2½ cups finely chopped onion
2 oz. vegetable fat or oil	¼ cup vegetable fat or oil
8 oz. tomatoes, skinned and chopped	½ lb. tomatoes, skinned and chopped
2–3 cloves garlic, chopped finely	2–3 cloves garlic, chopped finely
½ tablespoon ground coriander	½ tablespoon ground coriander
1½ teaspoons ground cumin (jeera)	1½ teaspoons ground cumin (jeera)
1 teaspoon ground cardamom	1 teaspoon ground cardamom
1 teaspoon ground turmeric	1 teaspoon ground turmeric
¼–½ teaspoon chilli powder (or cayenne pepper)	¼–½ teaspoon chili powder (or cayenne pepper)
1 large potato, cubed (optional)	1 large potato, cubed (optional)
1½ teaspoons salt	1½ teaspoons salt
juice ½ small lemon	juice ½ small lemon

Remove any gristle from the meat and cut into 1-inch cubes. Pour the boiling water over the coconut, leave to cool and then squeeze out as much of the milk as possible and discard the coconut.
In a heatproof casserole, fry the onion in the fat until golden brown. Stir in the tomatoes, garlic, and spices and fry for 4–5 minutes. Add the meat and potato and continue frying until the red has disappeared. Stir in the coconut milk and salt, cover and simmer very gently on top for 1–1½ hours or until the meat is tender. Add a little water if the liquid has evaporated

too much. Stir in the lemon juice a few minutes before the end.

Serve with boiled rice (allow 12 oz. for 4 people), chutney, poppadums and sambals (side dishes).

TO COOK POPPADUMS: Drop poppadums into $\frac{1}{2}$ inch of hot oil in a frying pan when they will swell immediately. After a second or two turn over. Remove and drain.

Dubonnet terrine

(illustrated in colour on page 38)

This meat loaf can be served hot with a coating of mashed potato, cold coated with potato mayonnaise or unadorned, left in the terrine or turned out of the tin.

Cooking time (hot) 2 hours 20–25 minutes, *(cold)* 2 hours.
Serves 8
Oven temperature 350° F., 180° C., Gas Mark 4
To serve hot 450–475° F., 230–240° C., Gas Mark 8–9
Size of tin: 9$\frac{1}{4}$ by 5$\frac{1}{4}$ by 2$\frac{3}{4}$ inch loaf tin, 7 inch cake tin, or 2$\frac{1}{2}$ pint (U.S. 3 pint) earthenware terrine.

IMPERIAL	AMERICAN
4 oz. streaky bacon rashers, finely cut (No. 4)	$\frac{1}{4}$ lb. bacon slices, finely cut
1 lb. lean pork	1 lb. lean pork
12 oz. calf or lamb liver	$\frac{3}{4}$ lb. calf or lamb liver
8 oz. onion, finely chopped	2 cups finely chopped onion
1 clove garlic, finely chopped and crushed	1 clove garlic, finely chopped and crushed
$\frac{3}{4}$ teaspoon marjoram	$\frac{3}{4}$ teaspoon marjoram
$\frac{3}{4}$ teaspoon savory	$\frac{3}{4}$ teaspoon savory
1$\frac{1}{2}$ teaspoons salt	1$\frac{1}{2}$ teaspoons salt
milled black pepper	freshly cracked black pepper
3–4 fl. oz. Dubonnet	scant $\frac{1}{4}$ cup Dubonnet
4 bay leaves	4 bay leaves

Cut off the rinds from the bacon and line the tin or terrine with the rashers. Put the pork and liver through a coarse mincer (or ask the butcher to do it for you). Mix in thoroughly the onion, garlic, herbs, salt and a good milling of black pepper. Stir in the Dubonnet and turn into prepared tin. Smooth the top evenly. Place the bay leaves along the top. Cover with foil and bake in a moderate oven for 2 hours.

TO SERVE HOT: Remove the meat to a heatproof dish. Strain the liquid from the tin into a measuring jug and make up to 1 pint (U.S. 2$\frac{1}{2}$ cups) with water. Bring to the boil in a saucepan, remove from the heat and stir in a large packet (5 oz.) of instant potato powder. Coat the loaf with it and decorate using a fork. Place in a very hot oven for 20–25 minutes until browned.

TO SERVE COLD: Pour away the liquid. Place a smaller tin on the top of the meat with a weight in it and leave until cold before turning out. If coating with potato, make up a large packet (5 oz.) of instant potato as instructed on the packet and leave to cool. Mix together 4 tablespoons (U.S. 5 tablespoons) mayonnaise, 2 tablespoons (U.S. 3 tablespoons) wine vinegar, 1 tablespoon boiling water, 1 tablespoon each chopped chives and parsley. Stir thoroughly into the potato and coat the loaf with it. Garnish with watercress if liked.

Birgit's roast pork

This is a Danish recipe given to me in Denmark, where they like to serve it with pickled cabbage and caramelized potatoes.

Cooking time 2$\frac{1}{2}$ hours
Oven temperature 350° F., 180° C., Gas Mark 4

IMPERIAL	AMERICAN
4 lb. loin of pork, with crackling	4 lb. loin of pork, with crackling
salt	salt
peppercorns	peppercorns
cloves	cloves
bay leaves	bay leaves

Ask the butcher to score the fat in narrow ribs downwards and then across about 2 inches apart. Rub all over well with salt, then stick into the ribs of fat (in lines less than an inch apart) the peppercorns, cloves and pieces of bay leaves, alternately. Stand the joint on a grid in a baking tin containing $\frac{1}{4}$–$\frac{1}{2}$ inch of water and baste with the water frequently. Roast in a moderate oven allowing 30 minutes per pound plus 30 minutes over.

Pour off most of the fat from the top of the liquid and use the rest for gravy.

Grilled steak à la Bergman

Ingrid Bergman is one of the finest actresses and one of the most fascinating women that I have had the privilege of meeting. Over lunch, we ranged the world, and then settled on cooking, over which she had definite opinions. She and her family are mad about herbs, so here is her favourite recipe for steak. Rub seasoning and finely chopped fresh herbs – dill, basil, marjoram, thyme and savory – into the steak. Brush it well with oil and grill both sides to your own taste of rare to well done, then sprinkle with lots more of the chopped herbs before serving.

Ceylon beef curry (see page 47)

Lamb pillau

This is an attractive dish for a buffet party because it can be heated through in the oven covered with foil.

For a party increase the quantities as desired, and chicken may be used in place of the lamb if preferred. Turn the rice mixture on to a large dish in a big mound. Scatter the fried onion all over the top and garnish with slices of hard-boiled eggs, and green peppers cut into thin rings. It looks exotic.

Cooking time 1 hour 28–32 minutes. *Serves* 4

Part 1 – Meat

IMPERIAL	AMERICAN
1½ lb. best and middle neck of lamb	1½ lb. rib roast of lamb
2 cardamoms	2 cardamoms
3 cloves	3 cloves
5 peppercorns	5 peppercorns
½ clove garlic	½ clove garlic
1 teaspoon salt	1 teaspoon salt
water	water

Cut the joints into cutlets and remove the outer skin. Turn into a saucepan with the rest of the ingredients and cover with water. Bring to the boil, skim, and simmer, covered, for 1 hour. Strain, keep the stock and allow it to get cold, then remove the solid fat from the top. Trim any excess fat from the meat, then cut the meat from the bones and cut into 1-inch pieces.

Part 2 – Rice

IMPERIAL	AMERICAN
3 oz. butter	6 tablespoons butter
1 tablespoon oil	1 tablespoon oil
2 oz. onion, chopped finely	½ cup finely chopped onion
1 clove garlic, chopped finely	1 clove garlic, chopped finely
1-inch stick cinnamon	1-inch stick cinnamon
4 cardamoms	4 cardamoms
3 cloves	3 cloves
1 bay leaf	1 bay leaf
12 oz. long grain rice	1¾ cups long grain rice
1¼ pints lamb stock	3 cups lamb stock
1½ teaspoons salt	1½ teaspoons salt
1½–2 oz. blanched almonds or cashew nuts	⅓–½ cup blanched almonds or cashew nuts
1 oz. sultanas	3 tablespoons seedless white raisins
5–6 oz. onion, sliced finely OR use bought crisp fried onion in packets (1½–2 oz.)	2 small onions, sliced finely OR use bought crisp fried onion in packets (1½–2 oz.)

In a heatproof casserole, melt 2 oz. (U.S. ¼ cup) of the butter with the oil and fry the chopped onion, garlic, cinnamon, cardamoms, cloves and bay leaf broken in half, until the onion is soft but not coloured. Add the rice and continue frying for 3–4 minutes stirring continuously. Pour in the stock and bring to the boil. Add the salt, cover the pan with a piece of cloth and then the lid and simmer very gently for 20–30 minutes, or until all the liquid is absorbed and the grains are separate.

Meanwhile, fry the nuts and sultanas gently in the rest of the butter, stirring, until the nuts are a light golden colour. Remove and add the sliced onions (adding a little more fat if necessary) and fry to a rich brown. Drain on kitchen paper to dry off.

As soon as the rice is cooked, gently stir in the meat, nuts and sultanas with a fork, and sprinkle the fried onion over the top.

Chilita beef casserole

(illustrated in colour on page 52)

Argentina – from where this recipe stems – exports some beautiful beef off the bone. Use any of their stewing cuts for this dish. If you choose home grown beef, I suggest the following:

Cooking time 2¾–3 hours. *Serves* 4

IMPERIAL	AMERICAN
1½ lb. chuck steak or top rump	1½ lb. boneless beef, chuck or rump
6 oz. streaky (belly) pork	⅓ lb. picnic shoulder pork
1 tablespoon oil	1 tablespoon oil
8 oz. onion, sliced coarsely	½ lb. onions, sliced coarsely
½ beef stock cube	½ beef bouillon cube
1 (8 oz.) can tomatoes	1 (8 oz.) can tomatoes
1 (8 oz.) can baked beans in tomato sauce	1 (8 oz.) can baked beans in tomato sauce
1 teaspoon caraway seeds	1 teaspoon caraway seeds
½ teaspoon ground fenugreek	½ teaspoon ground fenugreek
½ teaspoon salt	½ teaspoon salt
milled black pepper	freshly cracked black pepper

Cut the beef into large cubes and the pork into ¼–½ inch wide slices. Fry the pork in the oil until it begins to brown. Add the onion, cover the pan and cook over a medium heat for 5–7 minutes. Add the beef and fry gently uncovered, until all the red has disappeared. Stir in the crumbled beef cube, turn into a casserole and add the rest of the ingredients. Cover and simmer gently in the oven for 2½–3 hours or until the beef is tender.

Steak à la Karlin

Miriam Karlin is a comedienne-actress beloved by all because she is such fun off stage as well as on. She told me she thought she had had one of the first auto-timed ovens in London 'It's heaven for a working girl like me.' Her 'spiffing' party dish is this steak.

Cooking time 1 hour 5 minutes–1 hour 35 minutes. *Serves* 4

IMPERIAL	AMERICAN
$1\frac{1}{2}$ lb. rump or sirloin steak, in one piece	$1\frac{1}{2}$ lb. sirloin, rump or other good quality steak, in one piece
2 tablespoons corn oil	3 tablespoons corn oil
5 fl. oz. red wine	$\frac{2}{3}$ cup red wine
1 tablespoon vinegar	1 tablespoon vinegar
$\frac{3}{4}$ teaspoon chopped basil or mixed herbs	$\frac{3}{4}$ teaspoon chopped basil or mixed herbs
salt, milled black pepper	salt, freshly cracked black pepper
8–12 oz. tomatoes	$\frac{1}{2}$–$\frac{3}{4}$ lb. tomatoes
4 oz. mushrooms	1 cup mushrooms
1 large (7–8 oz.) or 2 small green peppers	1 large or 2 small sweet green peppers
2 cloves garlic	2 cloves garlic
1 stick celery (optional)	1 stalk celery (optional)
1 oz. flaked almonds, toasted	$\frac{1}{4}$ cup toasted, slivered almonds

Marinate the meat in the oil, wine, vinegar, herbs, and salt and pepper for several hours.
Skin and chop the tomatoes, wash and slice the mushrooms, deseed the pepper and slice the flesh, chop and crush the garlic and slice the celery if used. Turn all the vegetables into a saucepan and sweat, covered, for 5 minutes, stirring occasionally. Place the meat in a casserole and pour over the liquid in which it was marinated, and the vegetables and almonds. Season to taste. Cover and simmer in the oven for 1–$1\frac{1}{2}$ hours or until the steak is tender.
Place the steak on a hot dish and pour over the vegetable mixture. Slice to serve.

Casserole de foie

The fabulous French singer Juliette Greco used to enjoy cooking when she had time. Why? 'Because I am a Frenchwoman and I think we are just born with a knowledge of how to cook – here,' she said, pointing to her heart. She likes 'not simple' food, with vegetables such as onions, aubergines and tomatoes stewed to a pulp with herbs. She likes calf's liver cooked this way.

Cooking time 1–$1\frac{1}{4}$ hours. *Serves* 4

IMPERIAL	AMERICAN
12 oz.–1 lb. sliced calf's liver	$\frac{3}{4}$–1 lb. sliced calf liver
8–10 oz. onion, sliced lengthways	2 medium onions, sliced lengthwise
1 oz. butter	2 tablespoons butter
1 tablespoon olive oil	1 tablespoon olive oil
5 fl. oz. water	$\frac{2}{3}$ cup water
2 teaspoons fresh tarragon (or 1 teaspoon dried)	2 teaspoons fresh tarragon (or 1 teaspoon dried)
1 teaspoon thyme	1 teaspoon thyme
1 teaspoon salt	1 teaspoon salt
milled black pepper	freshly cracked black pepper

Cut away any gristle and skin from the liver. In a heatproof casserole, fry the onions in the butter and oil slowly, until golden. Add the liver and continue frying for 2–3 minutes each side. Stir in the water, chopped herbs and seasonings, and simmer slowly in the oven or on top for 50–60 minutes.

Spicy lamb stew

Cooking time 1 hour 10 minutes. *Serves* 4

IMPERIAL	AMERICAN
8 lamb cutlets, or $1\frac{1}{2}$ lb. middle and scrag end of neck	8 lamb rib chops, or $1\frac{1}{2}$ lb. rack of lamb
4 oz. carrots	$\frac{1}{4}$ lb. carrots
1 large or 2 small sticks celery	1 large or 2 small stalks celery
2 leeks	2 leeks
4–5 oz. onion, coarsely chopped	about 1 cup coarsely chopped onion
2 tablespoons oil	3 tablespoons oil
1 beef stock cube	1 beef bouillon cube
1 tablespoon flour	1 tablespoon all-purpose flour
1-inch stick cinnamon	1-inch stick cinnamon
3 cloves	3 cloves
$\frac{1}{2}$ bay leaf	$\frac{1}{2}$ bay leaf
$\frac{1}{2}$ teaspoon mixed herbs	$\frac{1}{2}$ teaspoon mixed herbs
12 fl. oz. water	$1\frac{1}{3}$ cups water
salt, pepper	salt, pepper

Pull off any outer skin from the cutlets and trim off excess fat. Place in a casserole. Wash the vegetables and slice the carrots, slice the celery finely and the leeks into $\frac{1}{2}$-inch pieces.
Fry onion in the oil until it begins to colour, add other vegetables and continue frying for 5–6 minutes until they begin to soften. Crumble beef cube into the pan, sprinkle over the flour and stir in. Add spices, herbs and water; bring to the boil, stirring. Season. Pour over cutlets, cover and simmer in the oven for 1 hour or until tender. Remove cinnamon.

Chilita beef casserole
(see page 50)

Guernsey tomato
and mushroom flan
(see page 66)

Barbecued pork chops

Cooking time 1 hour 5 minutes–1 hour 25 minutes. *Serves* 4

IMPERIAL	AMERICAN
4 spare rib chops, or belly of pork cut in pieces (1½–2 lb.)	4 spare rib pork chops
½ oz. lard	1 tablespoon lard
5 tablespoons tomato ketchup	6 tablespoons tomato catsup
2 tablespoons vinegar	3 tablespoons vinegar
2 tablespoons tarragon vinegar	3 tablespoons tarragon vinegar
4 tablespoons water	⅓ cup water
½ tablespoon soy sauce	½ tablespoon soy sauce
½–1 oz. onion, chopped finely	2 tablespoons finely chopped onion
½ teaspoon celery seeds	½ teaspoon celery seeds
1 bay leaf, crumbled	1 bay leaf, crumbled
½ teaspoon ground ginger	½ teaspoon ground ginger
1 oz. seedless raisins	3 tablespoons seedless raisins

In a heatproof casserole (or fry in a frying pan and then transfer to a casserole), gently brown the meat in the lard. Mix remaining ingredients and pour over the meat. Cover and simmer very gently for 1–1½ hours, or until the meat is tender.

NOTE: If belly is used, it is best made the day before serving and left in a cold place, so that the fat can be lifted off easily.

Wendy's baked gammon

The piquant and fascinating Wendy Craig, star of television and screen, hasn't much time for fancy cooking with a family to run as well as a career, so this is the glamorous dish she gives her guests 'which needs so little work, you see'.

Cooking time 1¾–2 hours. *Serves* 6
Oven temperature 325° F., 170° C., Gas Mark 3

IMPERIAL	AMERICAN
3–4 lb. middle gammon or forehock	3–4 lb. cured ham, with rind
½ bay leaf	½ bay leaf
4 peppercorns, crushed cloves	4 peppercorns, crushed cloves
1 (1 lb.) can pineapple chunks	1 (1 lb.) can pineapple chunks
4 oz. brown sugar	½ cup brown sugar
miniature bottle rum	miniature bottle rum

Cover the gammon with unsalted water and bring to the boil. Skim well, add bay leaf and peppercorns, cover, and simmer allowing 15 minutes per pound. Rip off the skin. Place in a roasting tin, score the fat into diamond shapes and stick a clove into the centre of each. Drain the pineapple chunks. Mix the juice with the sugar and rum and pour over the gammon. Bake for 1 hour, basting occasionally. Add the pineapple chunks for the last 10–15 minutes.

Tripe de Manio

Food is high on the list of priorities for the well known radio personality Jack de Manio, but he never weighs anything. 'I throw in everything I think of and it usually tastes absolutely splendid.' For more conventional cooks I discovered the necessary weights!

Cooking time 1¾–2¼ hours. *Serves* 4

IMPERIAL	AMERICAN
1¼–1½ lb. prepared tripe	1¼–1½ lb. fresh prepared tripe
4 oz. mushrooms	1 cup mushrooms
5–6 oz. onion, chopped coarsely	1¼–1½ cups coarsely chopped onion
1 clove garlic, chopped finely	1 clove garlic, chopped finely
2 tablespoons olive oil	3 tablespoons olive oil
1 lb. tomatoes, skinned and chopped	1 lb. tomatoes, skinned and chopped
1 teaspoon chopped parsley	1 teaspoon chopped parsley
½ teaspoon chopped marjoram	½ teaspoon chopped marjoram
½ teaspoon chopped basil	½ teaspoon chopped basil
5 fl. oz. chicken stock	⅔ cup chicken stock
4 tablespoons white wine	5 tablespoons white wine
1 teaspoon salt	1 teaspoon salt
good milling black pepper	freshly cracked black pepper

Blanch the tripe three or four times, by bringing it to the boil and renewing the water each time. Cut it into 1-inch squares. Wash the mushrooms and slice thinly, including stalks.
Fry the onion and garlic in the oil until soft but not coloured. Add the tripe, tomatoes and herbs, and fry gently for a few minutes. Transfer to a heatproof casserole or saucepan with the stock, wine and seasonings and allow to simmer gently for 1½–2 hours, according to the tripe used. Add the mushrooms after 1 hour.

Hot-sweet pork chops

Cooking time 12–14 minutes. *Serves 2*

IMPERIAL	AMERICAN
2 pork chops	2 pork chops
salt	salt
¼ teaspoon ground ginger	¼ teaspoon ground ginger
¼ teaspoon curry powder	¼ teaspoon curry powder
2 teaspoons grated orange rind	2 teaspoons grated orange rind
2 teaspoons made mustard	2 teaspoons prepared mustard
1–2 teaspoons honey	1–2 teaspoons honey

Cut off the skin and any excess fat from the chops. Sprinkle both sides with salt.
Mix the dry ingredients together, then make into a paste with the orange rind, mustard and honey. Spread half over one side of both chops and grill under medium heat for 6–7 minutes. Turn the chops over and repeat with the second side.

Pot roast hand of pork

This is a very economical and delicious joint. It is not only cheap to buy, but cheap to cook also as it requires only one ring or hot plate.

Cooking time 2 hours 35–40 minutes. *Serves 8–9*

IMPERIAL	AMERICAN
4½–5 lb. hand of pork	4½–5 lb. Boston butt of pork
salt	salt
2 oz. lard or dripping	¼ cup lard or meat drippings
good sprig of rosemary	good sprig of rosemary
1 bay leaf	1 bay leaf
1½–2 lb. peeled, mixed vegetables (onion, carrot, turnip, celery, etc.), cut in large pieces	1½–2 lb. peeled, mixed vegetables (onion, carrot, turnip, celery, etc.), cut in large pieces

Ask the butcher to score the rind deeply in fine ribs. Rub salt well all over into the joint. Melt the lard in a large, strong-bottomed saucepan and brown the meat all over in it. Add the rosemary and bay leaf, cover and reduce the heat. Cook gently for 1½ hours turning over the joint occasionally.
Lift out the joint, turn in the prepared vegetables, season, replace the meat on top and continue cooking for 1 hour, or until the meat and vegetables are tender.
Serve the meat, vegetables and gravy separately. Carve the meat, slicing from each end.

NOTE: The rind or fat of this joint will be rather tough. If it is desired crisp, place the joint under a medium grill for about 10 minutes until the crackling is a good brown.

Poultry and Game

Chicken Korma

Curry – in all its forms – is the national dish of India. There are literally hundreds of different kinds, Korma (a mild savoury curry) is typical of the North.

Cooking time 1 hour 10 minutes–1 hour 45 minutes. *Serves 4–5*

IMPERIAL	AMERICAN
2½–3 lb. chicken (dressed weight)	2½–3 lb. chicken (dressed weight)
1 pint soured cream or yogurt (solid curds in India)	2½ cups sour cream or yogurt (solid curds in India)
juice ½ lemon	juice ½ lemon
1½ teaspoons salt	1½ teaspoons salt
¼ teaspoon black pepper	¼ teaspoon black pepper
1½ oz. butter	3 tablespoons butter
1 tablespoon oil	1 tablespoon oil
6 oz. onion, sliced finely	1 medium onion, sliced finely
2 cloves garlic, chopped and crushed	2 cloves garlic, chopped and crushed
¼ teaspoon ground cloves	¼ teaspoon ground cloves
1½ tablespoons ground coriander	2 tablespoons ground coriander
1 tablespoon ground cardamom	1 tablespoon ground cardamom
1½ teaspoons finely chopped green (fresh) ginger, or ½ tablespoon ground ginger	1½ teaspoons finely chopped green (fresh) ginger, or ½ tablespoon ground ginger
1½ oz. ground almonds	⅓ cup ground almonds
½ oz. desiccated coconut	⅙ cup shredded coconut

Cut the chicken into neat joints and marinate them for 1 hour or more in the soured cream or yogurt, lemon juice, salt and pepper.
Melt the butter and oil together and fry the onion and garlic in it to a light golden colour. Then add the spices, ground almonds and coconut and continue frying gently for 3–4 minutes. Turn into a casserole, add the bird with the marinade. Cover and simmer very gently in the oven for 1–1½ hours until the chicken is tender. The gravy should be thick and should have no other liquid added to it. Serve with Pillau rice (see page 50 but omit the meat).

Sutherland steamed chicken

The exquisitely-voiced Joan Sutherland who charms the world with her singing, charmed me with her natural love of food as well. 'I love to cook a simple dish which I can just pop on the stove all together and forget. But it must have lots of onion and herbs mixed in,' she said. Here it is.

Cooking time 1½ hours. Serves 4–5

IMPERIAL	AMERICAN
3 lb. chicken (dressed weight)	3 lb. chicken (dressed weight)
salt, pepper	salt, pepper
½ teaspoon thyme	½ teaspoon thyme
½ teaspoon basil	½ teaspoon basil
½ teaspoon marjoram	½ teaspoon marjoram
1½ bay leaves	1½ bay leaves
8–10 oz. onion, sliced lengthways	1 large or 2 medium onions, sliced lengthwise
10 oz. long grain rice	scant 1½ cups long grain rice

Rub the chicken all over with salt and pepper and place it in a steamer. Mix the herbs, onion and ½ tablespoon salt with the rice and pack around the chicken. Steam steadily for 1½ hours, or until the chicken is tender.

Le lapin aux pruneaux

This is a Belgian dish I learned from the proprietor of a hotel in Le Zoute, which is unhappily now no more.

Cooking time 1½–1¾ hours. Serves 4–5

IMPERIAL	AMERICAN
2 lb. rabbit, cut into joints	2 lb. rabbit, cut into joints
¾ pint red wine	2 cups red wine
4 tablespoons wine vinegar	5 tablespoons wine vinegar
4–6 oz. onion, sliced	1 medium onion, sliced
8 peppercorns	8 peppercorns
2 bay leaves	2 bay leaves
1 large sprig thyme (or 1 teaspoon dried)	1 large sprig thyme (or 1 teaspoon dried)
salt, milled black pepper	salt, freshly cracked black pepper
12 oz. prunes, unsoaked	2 cups unsoaked prunes
1½ oz. flour	6 tablespoons all-purpose flour
1½ oz. butter	3 tablespoons butter
1 tablespoon oil	1 tablespoon oil
½ pint water	1¼ cups water
1 tablespoon gooseberry jam or redcurrant jelly	1 tablespoon gooseberry jam, or red currant jelly

Marinate the rabbit for 12–24 hours in ½ pint (U.S. 1¼ cups) of the wine, the vinegar, onion, peppercorns, bay leaves, thyme and ½ tablespoon salt. At the same time, soak the prunes in water.

Drain and dry the pieces of rabbit and shake them in a paper bag containing the flour, well seasoned with salt and pepper. Fry in the butter and oil until browned all over. Transfer to a casserole. Add the drained, stoned and halved prunes and the marinade from the rabbit with the rest of the wine and the water. Season, cover tightly and simmer gently in the oven for 1¼–1½ hours, or until the rabbit is tender. Remove from heat and stir in the jam or jelly.

Game puffs

These small puffs are an attractive way of finishing up a little left-over game.

Cooking time 7–9 minutes. Serves 4

IMPERIAL	AMERICAN
3 oz. cold game	scant ¼ lb. cold game
1 oz. ham	2 tablespoons chopped ham
2 oz. mushrooms	½ cup mushrooms
½ oz. butter	1 tablespoon butter
½ oz. flour	2 tablespoons all-purpose flour
5 fl. oz. game or chicken stock	⅔ cup game or chicken stock
¼ teaspoon ground mace	¼ teaspoon ground mace
bare ⅛ teaspoon cayenne pepper	bare ⅛ teaspoon cayenne pepper
salt, pepper	salt, pepper
8 oz. puff or flaky pastry (bought)	½ lb. puff paste (bought)

Chop the bird and ham into small pieces. Wash the mushrooms quickly and chop finely.

Melt the butter and sauté the mushrooms in it for a minute or two, stir in the flour until well blended, then add the stock and bring to the boil, stirring.

Boil for 1–2 minutes, remove and stir in the spices and meats, season with salt and pepper. Allow to get cold.

Roll out the pastry thinly on a floured board and cut into 12 circles with a 3½-inch pastry cutter. Place a tablespoon of the mixture on one half of each circle, brush round the edges with cold water, fold over to make half moons and seal the edges firmly. Leave for 30 minutes or so, then drop into hot deep fat (350°–380° F., 180°–190° C.), or fry in a frying pan, until a golden brown all over.

Turkey or chicken with cold curry sauce

This makes a very good dish for a buffet party. Lay largish pieces of bird on a flat dish sticking out irregularly and pour the sauce all over the centre but not to cover the bird completely. Garnish the dish with watercress.

Cooking time 25–30 minutes. Serves 8, or 4 as a main dish

IMPERIAL	AMERICAN
1 lb. flesh of roasted turkey or chicken (3¼–3½ lb. chicken roasted = 1 lb. flesh)	1 lb. flesh of roasted turkey, or chicken (3¼–3½ lb. chicken roasted = 1 lb. flesh)
2–3 oz. onion, sliced finely	1 small onion, sliced finely
1 oz. bird fat or butter	2 tablespoons bird fat or butter
½ tablespoon curry powder	½ tablespoon curry powder
¼ teaspoon turmeric	¼ teaspoon turmeric
1 oz. flour	¼ cup all-purpose flour
¾ pint chicken stock, or made with a stock cube	2 cups chicken stock, or made with a bouillon cube
1 tablespoon cranberry sauce or redcurrant jelly	1 tablespoon cranberry sauce or red currant jelly
5 fl. oz. double, single or soured cream	⅔ cup whipping, coffee, or sour cream

Fry the onion in the fat until soft and transparent. Add the curry powder and turmeric and continue frying for 3–4 minutes. Blend in the flour, then stir in the stock gradually and bring to the boil. Cover and simmer for 15–20 minutes. Remove, stir in the fruit sauce or jelly and rub through a sieve. When cold, stir in the cream.

Grouse or pigeon casserole with juniper

Cooking time 1½–2 hours. Serves 4

IMPERIAL	AMERICAN
2 large or 4 smaller grouse	2 large or 4 smaller grouse
1 oz. flour	¼ cup all-purpose flour
salt, milled black pepper	salt, freshly cracked black pepper
16–20 button onions	16–20 button onions
1 oz. butter	2 tablespoons butter
1 tablespoon oil	1 tablespoon oil
5 fl. oz. red wine	⅔ cup red wine
10 fl. oz. stock	1¼ cups stock
1 teaspoon chopped basil	1 teaspoon chopped basil
8 juniper berries	8 juniper berries
6 oz. mushrooms	1½ cups mushrooms

Coat the grouse with the flour, seasoned with salt and pepper. In a heatproof casserole (or after frying transfer to a casserole), fry the grouse and onions in the butter and oil until browned all over. Blend in the rest of the flour until smooth. Stir in the wine, stock, basil, crushed juniper berries (crush with the back of a spoon) and season with salt and milled black pepper. Cover and simmer in the oven for 1–1¼ hours, or until the birds are nearly tender; turning over the grouse occasionally. Add the washed mushrooms, left whole if small or sliced thickly, and continue cooking for 20–30 minutes.

Aylesbury game pie

(illustrated in colour on page 56)

This dish is traditionally eaten cold, but is also extremely good hot.

In ancient recipes, it was directed that the meat be placed 'in a large earthenware game pie-dish'. These dishes had special lids moulded to look like a pastry crust, and were brought to the table, thus entitling what is in fact a casserole, to be termed a 'pie'.

Cooking time 3½ hours. Serves 10–12
Oven temperatures 425° F., 220° C., Gas Mark 7 then 300–325° F., 150–170° C., Gas Mark 2–3

IMPERIAL	AMERICAN
1 hare	1 hare
2 lb. veal (or chicken or turkey meat)	2 lb. veal (or chicken or turkey meat)
1½ lb. sausage meat	1½ lb. sausage meat
1½ teaspoons thyme	1½ teaspoons thyme
½ teaspoon salt	½ teaspoon salt
milled black pepper	freshly cracked black pepper
2 bay leaves	2 bay leaves
6–8 oz. ham or bacon	about ½ lb. cured ham or Canadian style bacon
2 tablespoons brandy	3 tablespoons brandy
2 tablespoons water	3 tablespoons water

Remove all the flesh from the hare and cut it into pieces an inch or two in length. Cut the veal, free from skin and bone, in the same manner. Chop the liver and kidneys of the hare fairly finely and mix into the sausage meat with the thyme, salt and a good milling of pepper.

Place one bay leaf at the bottom of a 5-pint (U.S. 6-pint) casserole, then spread in layers, first the sausage meat, then the hare and veal mixed, seasoning to taste, lastly the ham. Repeat layers. Place the second bay leaf on top, pour in the brandy and water and cover the casserole with a lid. Make a flour and water paste and stick it round the rim to seal it, so that no steam can escape. Place the casserole in a hot oven for ½ hour, then lower the heat and continue cooking for a further 3 hours.

Aylesbury game pie (see opposite)

Cream turkey Aline

This is my mother's favourite way of finishing up the Christmas turkey.

Cooking time 5–6 minutes. Serves 4

IMPERIAL	AMERICAN
12 oz. cold turkey or chicken	¾ lb. cold turkey or chicken
2 oz. onion, chopped finely	½ cup finely chopped onion
1½ oz. bird fat or butter	3 tablespoons bird fat, or butter
1 oz. flour	¼ cup all-purpose flour
½ teaspoon ground ginger	½ teaspoon ground ginger
1 teaspoon chopped oregano	1 teaspoon chopped oregano
¾ pint turkey or chicken stock or milk	2 cups turkey or chicken stock, or milk
salt	salt
chopped parsley (optional)	chopped parsley (optional)

Slice the turkey (and use stuffing as well if there is any left) and lay in a shallow heatproof dish. Cover with foil and very gently heat through in the oven. In a small thick-bottomed saucepan, fry the onion in the fat until amber coloured. Blend in the flour, ginger and oregano until smooth. Pour in the stock or milk and bring to the boil, stirring with a wire whisk. Add salt to taste and boil for 2–3 minutes. Pour over the bird and serve sprinkled with chopped parsley, if liked, for colour.

Unwinese pigeon

It is a treat to eat with 'Professor' Stanley Unwin – that master of scrambled English.
'The anticipation of coming to lunch has been giving me deep joy in the drooly of the saliva glades' was his greeting! And he went on to enjoy his 'stuffle-down with a controlled burpy paradole'. This was his 'stuffle-down'.

Cooking time 1¾–2¼ hours. Serves 4

IMPERIAL	AMERICAN
2 large or 4 small pigeons	2 large or 4 small pigeons
2 oz. streaky bacon rashers	3 slices bacon
2 tablespoons corn oil	3 tablespoons corn oil
3–4 oz. onion, sliced	1 medium onion, sliced
½ oz. flour	2 tablespoons all-purpose flour
½ tablespoon tomato purée	½ tablespoon tomato paste
4 fl. oz. game or chicken stock	½ cup game or chicken stock
5 fl. oz. red wine	⅔ cup red wine
¾ teaspoon chopped rosemary	¾ teaspoon chopped rosemary
½ teaspoon salt	½ teaspoon salt
milled black pepper	freshly cracked black pepper

Cut large pigeons in halves along the backbones and cut the bacon into ½–¾-inch pieces. Fry the pigeons in the oil until lightly browned and transfer to a casserole. Fry the bacon and onion in the remaining oil until golden brown. Stir in the flour, tomato purée, liquids, rosemary and seasonings. Cover and simmer in the oven for 1½–2 hours, or until the pigeons are tender.

Poulet à l'estragon

Hardy Amies needs no introduction, men as well as women admire his unique styling in clothes. He prefers the simple English dishes such as cottage pie and fried fish for every day, but partywise his taste is for French food. 'I feel a bit cheaty about this. I don't create. I just add bits of something I think will be nice to a good standard recipe,' he told me. So here is his party piece.

Cooking time 1 hour 5–10 minutes. Serves 4
Oven temperature 450° F., 230° C., Gas Mark 8, then 350° F., 180° C., Gas Mark 4

IMPERIAL	AMERICAN
3 lb. roasting chicken (dressed weight)	3 lb. roasting chicken (dressed weight)
butter	butter
1–2 tablespoons chopped fresh tarragon (half quantity if dried)	1–3 tablespoons chopped fresh tarragon (half quantity if dried)
1 clove garlic, chopped and crushed	1 clove garlic, chopped and crushed
rock salt	coarse salt
milled black pepper	freshly cracked black pepper
lemon juice	lemon juice
2 tablespoons brandy	3 tablespoons brandy

Wash and wipe the inside of the bird well. Mash together 2 oz. (U.S. ¼ cup) butter with the tarragon, garlic, and salt and pepper to taste. Stuff into the bird. Rub softened butter all over the outside and season with salt, pepper and lemon juice.
Lay the bird on its side in a baking tin and roast in a very hot oven for 30 minutes, turning over once. Then turn it breast upwards and continue roasting at a moderate temperature for 30 minutes, basting with the butter melted from the bird. Pour away less than half the fat and pour the rest into a small saucepan with ½ pint (U.S. 1¼ cups) stock made from the giblets. Do not thicken. Heat through for gravy.
Pour the warm brandy over the chicken, set it alight and, when the flames have subsided, return to the oven for 5–10 minutes.
He usually serves this dish with new potatoes and a green salad.

Vegetables

Beetroot in sour cream salad

Serves 4

IMPERIAL	AMERICAN
1 lb. beetroot, cooked	1 lb. cooked beets
1 tablespoon chopped chives	1 tablespoon chopped chives
½ tablespoon chopped fresh tarragon or thyme (half quantity dried)	½ tablespoon chopped fresh tarragon, or thyme (half quantity dried)
5 fl. oz. soured cream or yogurt	⅔ cup sour cream or yogurt
salt, pepper	salt, pepper

Peel the beetroot and cut into ½-inch cubes. Stir the herbs into the soured cream and season highly with salt and pepper. Mix with the beetroot.

Cabbage with soured cream

Cooking time 6–8 minutes. Serves 4

IMPERIAL	AMERICAN
1½ lb. white cabbage	1½ lb. white cabbage
1½–2 oz. onion, chopped finely	about ½ cup finely chopped onion
5 fl. oz. water	⅔ cup water
½ teaspoon caraway seeds	½ teaspoon caraway seeds
1½ teaspoons salt	1½ teaspoons salt
milled black pepper	freshly cracked black pepper
1 tablespoon flour	1 tablespoon all-purpose flour
5 fl. oz. soured cream	⅔ cup sour cream

Cut out the hard stalk from the cabbage and shred leaves finely. Turn into a saucepan with the onion, water, caraway seeds and seasonings. Cover and boil for 5 minutes, turning over the cabbage once or twice.
Make a paste of the flour with the soured cream. Stir into the pan, bring again to the boil, stirring, and boil for 1–2 minutes.

Fennel and cucumber salad

Surround this salad with halved orange slices for serving with duck, goose or pork.

No cooking. Serves 4

IMPERIAL	AMERICAN
6–8 oz. fennel root	approx. ½ lb. fennel root
7–8 radishes	7–8 radishes
4 oz. unpeeled cucumber	¼ lb. unpeeled cucumber
1 tablespoon lemon juice	1 tablespoon lemon juice
2 tablespoons olive oil	3 tablespoons olive oil
salt, pepper	salt, pepper
½ teaspoon chopped fresh mint	½ teaspoon chopped fresh mint
chopped parsley or chives	chopped parsley or chives

Remove any discoloured piece from the fennel. Wash all the vegetables well and dry them. Cut the fennel into narrow strips, the radishes into thin slices and the cucumber into small cubes. Turn into a bowl.
Beat the lemon juice and oil together. Season well with salt and pepper and stir in the mint. Pour over the vegetables and turn them round in the dressing. Sprinkle with chopped parsley or chives to serve.

Rotkohl

This is an Austrian recipe culled from a Viennese journalist friend.

Cooking time 40–45 minutes. Serves 4–5

IMPERIAL	AMERICAN
1½ lb. red cabbage	1½ lb. red cabbage
1 medium cooking apple	1 medium baking apple
4 oz. onion, sliced thinly	1 medium onion, sliced thinly
1 tablespoon brown sugar	1 tablespoon brown sugar
1 oz. lard	2 tablespoons lard
5 fl. oz. red wine	⅔ cup red wine
4 tablespoons water	5 tablespoons water
1 teaspoon salt	1 teaspoon salt
milled black pepper	freshly cracked black pepper
½ teaspoon caraway seeds	½ teaspoon caraway seeds
3 cloves	3 cloves

Cut the cabbage into quarters and cut out the hard centre stalk. Shred finely. Peel, core and chop the apple coarsely.
Fry the onion and sugar in the lard until the onion is a golden brown. Add the rest of the ingredients, cover and simmer for 40–45 minutes, stirring occasionally.

Sautéed cucumber

Cooking time 8–10 minutes. Serves 4

IMPERIAL	AMERICAN
1 large cucumber	1 large cucumber
1 oz. butter	2 tablespoons butter
salt	salt
grated nutmeg	grated nutmeg

Peel the cucumber and cut into ½-inch dice. Sauté gently in the butter with the pan covered, stirring occasionally, until tender and lightly coloured, 8–10 minutes. Sprinkle with salt and nutmeg to serve.

Carrot salad

No cooking. Serves 4

IMPERIAL	AMERICAN
12 oz. young carrots	¾ lb. young carrots
10–12 spring onions	10–12 scallions
1 tablespoon vinegar	1 tablespoon vinegar
3 tablespoons olive or corn oil	4 tablespoons olive or corn oil
½ teaspoon salt	½ teaspoon salt
good milling pepper	freshly cracked black pepper
¼ teaspoon sugar	¼ teaspoon sugar
½ tablespoon chopped fresh burnet and dill mixed (or 1 teaspoon dried dill weed and savory)	½ tablespoon chopped fresh burnet and dill mixed (or 1 teaspoon dried dill weed and savory)
½ tablespoon chopped parsley	½ tablespoon chopped parsley

Peel the carrots and grate them on a grater.
Slice the onions very finely.
Beat the vinegar and oil together with the seasonings and herbs, except the parsley. Mix thoroughly with the carrot and onion and turn into a bowl. Sprinkle over the chopped parsley to serve.

Almonded button onions

Cooking time 27–32 minutes. Serves 4
Oven temperature 350° F., 180° C., Gas Mark 4

IMPERIAL	AMERICAN
1 lb. pickling or small onions	1 lb. pickling or small onions
2 oz. almonds, blanched and halved	½ cup blanched and halved almonds
1½ oz. butter	3 tablespoons butter
1½ teaspoons brown sugar	1½ teaspoons brown sugar
½ teaspoon salt	½ teaspoon salt
⅛ teaspoon each cayenne pepper, nutmeg, cloves	⅛ teaspoon each cayenne pepper, nutmeg, cloves

Peel the onions carefully and leave whole. Fry the almonds very gently in the butter until they begin to turn golden, 1–2 minutes. Blend in the sugar, salt and spices, then add the onions and turn around until well coated. Turn into a casserole, cover and bake in a moderate oven for 25–30 minutes, until just tender.

Potato mint casserole

This was a favourite dish of my husband's family and he always demanded it as soon as the new potatoes made their appearance each spring!
The quantities must depend upon the appetite of the family. This dish can be served as soup or it can form a main course.

Cooking time 15–20 minutes

Scrape small new potatoes and turn into a heatproof casserole or saucepan. Cover with milk and season with salt and pepper. Add a large quantity of mint sprays or leaves, enough to impregnate the milk and potatoes with the flavour. Bring to the boil and simmer gently for 15–20 minutes. Be careful that the milk does not overboil, it is best to keep the lid tipped up a little.
Serve in soup bowls.

Herbed marrow with green pepper

Cooking time 14–18 minutes. Serves 4

IMPERIAL	AMERICAN
2¼–2½ lb. marrow	2¼–2½ lb. marrow squash
1 (4 oz.) green pepper	1 sweet green pepper
3 oz. onion, sliced finely	1 small onion, sliced finely
1 oz. butter	2 tablespoons butter
1 teaspoon dill weed	1 teaspoon dill weed
¼–½ teaspoon mixed herbs	¼–½ teaspoon mixed herbs
¾ teaspoon garlic chips or minced, or 1 clove garlic crushed	¾ teaspoon garlic chips or minced, or 1 clove garlic crushed
1 teaspoon salt	1 teaspoon salt
milled black pepper	freshly cracked black pepper
4 tablespoons water	5 tablespoons water

Peel and cut the marrow into ¾-inch cubes. Wash the pepper, discard stalk and seeds and slice the flesh coarsely.
In a heatproof casserole, fry the onion and pepper in the butter for 3–4 minutes until lightly softened. Add the herbs, garlic, salt and pepper to taste and sweat, covered, for 3–4 minutes. Stir in the marrow and water and simmer gently, covered, for 8–10 minutes or until the marrow is only just tender.

Melons Alaska
(see page 70)

Date and
orange flan
(see page 71)

Broad beans with savory

In France, they boil every kind of green bean with sprigs of savory. For this I think winter savory is the better, as it has a more pungent flavour to withstand dilution by the water. But for addition to a sauce, the more subtle flavour of summer savory is preferable.

Cooking time 8–15 minutes. Serves 4

IMPERIAL	AMERICAN
2½ lb. broad beans (12–14 oz. podded)	2½ lb. lima or fava beans (12–14 oz. podded)
½ oz. butter	1 tablespoon butter
½ oz. flour	2 tablespoons flour
5 fl. oz. milk	⅔ cup milk
1 tablespoon chopped parsley	1 tablespoon chopped parsley
¾ teaspoon chopped fresh summer savory (or half quantity dried)	¾ teaspoon chopped fresh summer savory (or half quantity dried)
salt, pepper	salt, pepper

Drop the beans into boiling salted water and boil for 8–15 minutes (according to age), until tender. Drain.

Meanwhile make the sauce. Melt the butter, blend in the flour, add the milk and bring to the boil, stirring with a wire whisk. Boil for 2–3 minutes, remove from the heat, add the herbs and season. Mix in the beans.

Yellow rice

This is an attractive way of serving rice either with a curry, or with chicken, veal and fish dishes.

Cooking time 22–25 minutes. Serves 4

IMPERIAL	AMERICAN
1½ oz. butter	3 tablespoons butter
2 oz. onion, finely chopped	½ cup finely chopped onion
½ teaspoon turmeric	½ teaspoon turmeric
8 oz. long grain rice	generous 1 cup long grain rice
1 pint chicken stock	2½ cups chicken stock
¾ teaspoon salt	¾ teaspoon salt
1-inch stick cinnamon, broken in two	1-inch stick cinnamon, broken in two
5 cardamoms	5 cardamoms
6 cloves	6 cloves

Melt the butter in a heatproof casserole or thick bottomed saucepan, and fry the onion gently until soft but not coloured. Blend in the turmeric, then stir in the rice and fry slowly, stirring all the time, for 3–4 minutes. Add the stock, salt and spices and bring to the boil. Stir once, lower the heat to simmering, cover with a lid and allow to simmer for 15–17 minutes. Test the rice between the teeth, if not tender enough (it should still be a little firm in the centre) and the liquid not completely absorbed, allow to cook longer. Turn into a bowl, fluff up with a fork.

Sauces

Sauce béarnaise

Cooking time 5–8 minutes. Serves 3–4

IMPERIAL	AMERICAN
½ teaspoon finely chopped shallot	½ teaspoon finely chopped shallot
½ teaspoon chopped tarragon	½ teaspoon chopped tarragon
1 teaspoon chopped chervil	1 teaspoon chopped chervil
½ teaspoon salt	½ teaspoon salt
milling black pepper	freshly cracked black pepper
⅛ teaspoon cayenne pepper	⅛ teaspoon cayenne pepper
2 tablespoons tarragon vinegar or 1 tablespoon tarragon vinegar and 1 tablespoon white wine	3 tablespoons tarragon vinegar or 1½ tablespoons tarragon vinegar and 1½ tablespoons white wine
2 large egg yolks	2 large egg yolks
3 oz. butter	6 tablespoons butter

Turn the shallot, tarragon, chervil, seasonings and liquid into a small saucepan and bubble until reduced by two-thirds. Remove from the heat and allow to cool a little. Stir in the egg yolks. Replace on a very gentle heat and beat in the butter piece by piece, until the sauce is thick and smooth.

Tartare sauce

No cooking. Serves 4

IMPERIAL	AMERICAN
1 teaspoon finely chopped chives or onion	1 teaspoon finely chopped chives or onion
1½ teaspoons chopped capers	1½ teaspoons chopped capers
1½ teaspoons chopped gherkins	1½ teaspoons chopped sour dill pickle
¼ teaspoon chopped chervil	¼ teaspoon chopped chervil
¼ teaspoon chopped tarragon	¼ teaspoon chopped tarragon
few drops lemon juice	few drops lemon juice
¼ pint mayonnaise	⅔ cup mayonnaise

Mix all the ingredients into the mayonnaise.

Cold barbecue sauce

This cold barbecue sauce is especially good with grilled or fried fish, chicken, hamburgers, beef-burgers, and with raw vegetables. It can also be served warm (but not hot), if preferred, or can be kept in a cold place or a refrigerator for many days.

No cooking. Serves 7–8

IMPERIAL	AMERICAN
8 tablespoons mayonnaise	$\frac{2}{3}$ cup mayonnaise
4 tablespoons tomato ketchup	5 tablespoons tomato catsup
1–2 teaspoons lemon juice (depending upon the mayonnaise)	1–2 teaspoons lemon juice (depending upon the mayonnaise)
1 teaspoon Worcestershire sauce	1 teaspoon Worcestershire sauce
1 teaspoon grated onion	1 teaspoon grated onion
1 teaspoon curry powder	1 teaspoon curry powder
$\frac{1}{2}$ teaspoon ground cumin	$\frac{1}{2}$ teaspoon ground cumin
$\frac{1}{4}$ teaspoon chilli powder or cayenne pepper	$\frac{1}{2}$ teaspoon chili powder or cayenne pepper
1 teaspoon salt	1 teaspoon salt

Beat everything together thoroughly.

Béchamel sauce

A real Béchamel sauce has infinitely more flavour than the butter, flour and milk concoction which often passes under the guise of Béchamel, instead of plain 'white sauce'. Without the vegetables and spices, it cannot form a satisfactory substitute when true Béchamel is called for.

Cooking time 10 minutes, *plus* 30 minutes *to infuse milk*

IMPERIAL	AMERICAN
2 oz. onion, quartered	1 small onion, quartered
$1\frac{1}{2}$–2 oz. carrots, chopped	2 small carrots, chopped
1 oz. celery, chopped	1 stalk celery, chopped
$\frac{1}{2}$ bay leaf	$\frac{1}{2}$ bay leaf
2 cloves	2 cloves
4 peppercorns, slightly crushed	4 peppercorns, slightly crushed
$\frac{1}{8}$ teaspoon ground mace	$\frac{1}{8}$ teaspoon ground mace
1 teaspoon salt	1 teaspoon salt
1 pint milk	$2\frac{1}{2}$ cups milk
$1\frac{1}{2}$ oz. butter	3 tablespoons butter
$1\frac{1}{2}$ oz. flour	6 tablespoons all-purpose flour

Bring the first 8 ingredients to the boil in the milk. Remove from the heat, cover and allow to infuse for at least 30 minutes, then strain. Melt the butter, blend in the flour, add the strained milk and bring to the boil stirring with a wire whisk. Boil for a minute or two. A little cream may now be added if desired. Adjust seasoning and bring again to the boil.

VARIATION: Quick method. If time does not permit for the preparation of the vegetables, a milder flavoured sauce can be made by sticking 3 cloves into an onion and standing the onion in the milk, to infuse with the other seasonings. Then proceed.

Mint and apple jelly

For those who prefer a slightly sweeter mint accompaniment to their lamb than the traditional sharp mint sauce, this is a very popular jelly.

Cooking time 17–20 minutes

IMPERIAL	AMERICAN
1 lb. tart cooking apples (bramley seedlings are best)	1 lb. baking apples
$\frac{1}{2}$ pint malt vinegar	$1\frac{1}{4}$ cups malt vinegar
1 lb. granulated sugar	1 lb. sugar
4 (well packed) tablespoons chopped, fresh mint	5 (well packed) tablespoons chopped, fresh mint

Wash and chop the unpeeled apples roughly, removing the seeds. Cover and boil with the vinegar until the apples are soft, about 10 minutes. Rub through a sieve. Return the pulp to the saucepan with the sugar, bring to the boil stirring, and boil fast for 7–9 minutes until a set is obtained. Remove from the heat, stir in the mint and a few drops of green food colouring if desired.
Pour into warm bottles and cover immediately.
Makes 2 lb.

Horseradish sauce

This is a good accompaniment to roast or boiled beef, fried or grilled fish, and with baked potatoes or beetroot.

IMPERIAL	AMERICAN
1–2 tablespoons finely grated fresh horseradish, or double quantity of bottled horseradish cream	1–3 tablespoons finely grated fresh horseradish, or double quantity of bottled horseradish cream
$\frac{1}{2}$ pint Béchamel sauce (quick method, above)	$1\frac{1}{4}$ cups Béchamel sauce (quick method, above)
$\frac{1}{2}$ teaspoon lemon juice	$\frac{1}{2}$ teaspoon lemon juice
1–2 tablespoons cream	1–3 tablespoons cream
salt, pepper	salt, pepper

Mix horseradish into the sauce to the strength you desire, add the lemon juice and cream and season fairly highly. Heat through.

Long life mint sauce

This sauce will keep indefinitely in a cupboard or a dark place.

Cooking time 3 minutes

IMPERIAL	AMERICAN
8 oz. granulated sugar	generous 1 cup sugar
1 pint white malt vinegar	2½ cups white malt vinegar
4 oz. chopped mint	¼ lb. chopped mint
(spearmint or apple mint)	(spearmint or apple mint)

Bring the sugar and vinegar to the boil, stirring until the sugar is completely dissolved. Boil for 3 minutes then pour at once on to the mint. Leave, covered, until cold.
Pour into (preferably) dark coloured bottles.

Tarragon vinegar

The best time to make this vinegar – or any herb vinegar – is to pick the leaves as soon as the flower buds appear on the plant, but before they begin to open.
Pack a glass jar full of leaves. Fill the jar with white wine vinegar, cover and leave to infuse for two weeks. Strain and pour into bottles. A branch of tarragon put into each bottle makes it look glamorous and also increases the strength of the vinegar.

VARIATIONS: Any of the following vinegars – and any other you may like – can be made in exactly the same way: basil, burnet, marjoram, mint, mixed herbs.

Neapolitan tomato sauce

(illustrated in colour on page 64)

A thick tomato sauce is particularly good with spaghetti, macaroni, Tournedos, or any meat requiring a piquant sauce.

Cooking time 20–30 minutes. *Serves 3–4 according to use*

IMPERIAL	AMERICAN
1 large clove garlic	1 large clove garlic
4 tablespoons olive oil	5 tablespoons olive oil
1 onion, chopped	1 onion, chopped
2 tablespoons tomato purée	3 tablespoons tomato paste
2 tablespoons warm water	3 tablespoons warm water
1 (14 oz.) can tomatoes	1 (14 oz.) can tomatoes
flesh ½ small green pepper, chopped	flesh ½ small sweet green pepper, chopped
½ teaspoon basil	½ teaspoon basil
½ teaspoon marjoram	½ teaspoon marjoram
small sprig rosemary (optional)	small sprig rosemary (optional)
1 bay leaf	1 bay leaf
½ teaspoon sugar	½ teaspoon sugar
½ teaspoon salt	½ teaspoon salt
good milling black pepper	freshly cracked black pepper

Crush the clove of garlic without cutting it and heat in the oil without browning. Remove the garlic and sauté the chopped onion in the oil. Dilute the tomato purée with the warm water and add to the oil with the contents of the can of tomatoes (cut the tomatoes roughly removing the cores) and the rest of the ingredients. Bring to the boil and simmer, uncovered, for 20–30 minutes, stirring occasionally. Remove the rosemary and bay leaf before serving.

Créole sauce

The original and perennial sarong girl, Dorothy Lamour, whose vital statistics have not changed one inch since she first wowed the public in her sarong, gave me this recipe for her standby sauce. She usually makes about three times this quantity and keeps the rest in her freezer to use 'with chicken, veal, shellfish or anything. It's so handy when folk drop in,' she explained.

Cooking time 1½–1¾ hours. *Serves 4–5*

IMPERIAL	AMERICAN
1 (4 oz.) green pepper	1 sweet green pepper
4 oz. onion, peeled	1 medium onion, peeled
1 large clove garlic	1 large clove garlic
½ oz. butter	1 tablespoon butter
½ tablespoon corn oil	½ tablespoon corn oil
1 (14 oz.) can tomatoes	1 (14 oz.) can tomatoes
1 tablespoon tomato purée	1 tablespoon tomato paste
1 bay leaf	1 bay leaf
½ teaspoon chopped oregano	½ teaspoon chopped oregano
¼ teaspoon chopped thyme	¼ teaspoon chopped thyme
½ teaspoon salt	½ teaspoon salt
good milling black pepper	freshly cracked black pepper
1½ teaspoons sugar	1½ teaspoons sugar

Wash the pepper, discard the stalk and seeds and chop the flesh coarsely. Chop the onion about the same size and the garlic very finely. In a large thick-bottomed saucepan, fry the onions in the butter and oil until amber coloured. Add the pepper and garlic and continue frying for 4–5 minutes. Stir in the rest of the ingredients. Bring to the boil and simmer, covered, for 1¼–1½ hours, stirring occasionally.

Neapolitan tomato sauce (see opposite)

Savoury Supper and Snack Dishes

Guernsey tomato and mushroom flan

(illustrated in colour on page 52)

Grated cheese or chopped ham can be added, as an exciting variation, to this tasty, light luncheon or supper dish.

Cooking time 35–40 minutes. Serves 4
Oven temperature 400° F., 200° C., Gas Mark 6

IMPERIAL	AMERICAN
1 lb. tomatoes	1 lb. tomatoes
4 oz. mushrooms	1 cup mushrooms
2–3 oz. onion, finely sliced	1 small onion, finely sliced
1 oz. butter	2 tablespoons butter
¼ teaspoon basil	¼ teaspoon basil
¼ teaspoon savory	¼ teaspoon savory
2 large eggs	2 large eggs
salt, pepper	salt, pepper
lightly baked 7-inch flan case	lightly baked 7-inch pie shell
sprigs parsley (optional)	sprigs parsley (optional)

Skin the tomatoes, by dropping them into boiling water for a few seconds and then plunging them at once into cold water. Cut some into neat slices as garnish and keep aside. Chop the rest fairly finely. Wash the mushrooms quickly. Reserve one good one and cut the rest, unpeeled, into thick slices, including the stalks. Cut each slice into 2 or 3 pieces.
Fry the onion in the butter until golden. Add the mushrooms and continue cooking gently for 3–4 minutes. Remove from the heat and stir in the chopped tomato, herbs and well beaten eggs. Season well with salt and pepper, and pour into the flan case.
Bake in a moderate oven for 20 minutes, then place the reserved mushroom in the centre and the tomato slices all around and continue baking for a further 15–20 minutes.
To serve, garnish with sprigs of parsley or finely chopped parsley, if liked.

Omelette aux fines herbes

This is the favourite French omelette and really does require fresh herbs.

Cooking time 2–3 minutes. Serves 2

IMPERIAL	AMERICAN
4 eggs	4 eggs
1–1½ tablespoons chopped fresh parsley, chives, chervil and tarragon, mixed	1–2 tablespoons chopped fresh parsley, chives, chervil and tarragon, mixed
salt, pepper	salt, pepper
½ oz. butter	1 tablespoon butter

Break the eggs into a basin, add the herbs and a pinch of salt and pepper. Beat them with a fork only long enough to blend the yolks and whites. Use a 7-inch base omelette pan and place it on a gentle heat to let it heat slowly, so that it is uniformly hot all over. Now add the butter and heat. When it foams and begins to smoke slightly, but before it turns colour, pour in the eggs. Stir them with a fork rather as if you were making scrambled eggs and, when they begin to set, lift the edges to allow any liquid still left to run underneath.
As soon as the mixture has set lightly (it will continue to cook as in scrambled eggs) but is still creamy on top, draw the pan away from the heat, tilt it away from you and fold the omelette over quickly. Or it can be rolled. Turn out on to a hot plate and serve immediately. The whole process should not take more than 2–3 minutes. Lightly draw a piece of butter across the top to give it a glaze.

Macaroni cheese special

Cooking time 48–53 minutes. Serves 4–5
Oven temperature 350° F., 180° C., Gas Mark 4

IMPERIAL	AMERICAN
8 oz. cut macaroni	2 cups cut macaroni
6 oz. Cheddar cheese, cubed	1 cup cubed Cheddar cheese
1–1½ oz. onion, very finely chopped	¼–⅓ cup finely chopped onion
8 oz. tomatoes, skinned and chopped	½ lb. tomatoes, skinned and chopped
1 teaspoon basil or oregano	1 teaspoon basil or oregano
2 oz. bacon rashers, chopped	3 bacon slices, chopped
1 oz. butter	2 tablespoons butter
2 eggs	2 eggs
½ pint milk	1½ cups milk
¼–½ teaspoon paprika pepper (optional)	¼–½ teaspoon paprika pepper (optional)
grated cheese	grated cheese
dried breadcrumbs	fine dry bread crumbs

Drop the macaroni into boiling, salted water and boil for 7–8 minutes until it is just tender; stirring for the first two or three minutes to stop it sticking to the bottom. Drain.

In a casserole greased round the sides, place alternate layers of macaroni and the cubed cheese, onion, tomato, herb and bacon, finishing with macaroni. Dot each layer with flakes of butter. Beat the eggs with the milk and paprika, if used, and pour into the casserole. Sprinkle the top with grated cheese and breadcrumbs mixed and bake in a moderate oven for 40–45 minutes.

Spaghetti Caruso

This is a dish Enrico Caruso, the great Italian tenor, used to enjoy enormously and which has been named after him. He was a great gourmet so he probably liked far more spaghetti than the quantity given here. But this amount is usually ample for more ordinary appetites.

Cooking time 20–25 minutes. *Serves* 4

IMPERIAL	AMERICAN
1 (6–8 oz.) red or green pepper	1 large sweet red or green pepper
3 cloves garlic	3 cloves garlic
2 tablespoons olive oil	3 tablespoons olive oil
1 (1 lb.) can tomatoes	1 (1 lb.) can tomatoes
1 teaspoon chopped basil	1 teaspoon chopped basil
1 tablespoon chopped parsley	1 tablespoon chopped parsley
$1\frac{1}{2}$ teaspoons salt	$1\frac{1}{2}$ teaspoons salt
milled black pepper	freshly cracked black pepper
$\frac{1}{4}$–$\frac{1}{2}$ teaspoon sugar	$\frac{1}{4}$–$\frac{1}{2}$ teaspoon sugar
8 oz. courgettes	$\frac{1}{2}$ lb. small zucchini
$1\frac{1}{2}$ oz. flour	6 tablespoons all-purpose flour
12 oz. spaghetti	$\frac{3}{4}$ lb. spaghetti
1–$1\frac{1}{2}$ oz. butter	2–3 tablespoons butter
grated Parmesan cheese	grated Parmesan cheese

Remove the stalk and seeds from the pepper and cut the flesh into $\frac{1}{4}$-inch pieces. Cut the garlic into halves and, with a fork, squash round in the bottom of pan in the oil while it is heating, then remove. Fry the pepper gently in the oil for 3–4 minutes, then add the tomatoes (removing the hard cores), herbs, seasonings and sugar. Cover the pan and allow to simmer for 15–20 minutes.

Slice the unpeeled courgettes about $\frac{1}{8}$ inch in thickness, shake the slices in the flour, seasoned with salt and pepper, in a paper bag until they are well coated. Shake off surplus and fry in more oil until brown on both sides. Drain on absorbent paper.

Meanwhile cook the spaghetti. Hold it in a bundle and first lower the ends into boiling salted water in a large pan, then gradually wind the rest round the inside of the pan as it becomes supple enough to bend. Boil for 10–12 minutes until just tender (al dente). Drain, return to the pan in which you have melted the butter and turn around until the spaghetti is coated. Turn the spaghetti on to a hot dish, pour over the sauce. Sprinkle lavishly with grated Parmesan and arrange the courgettes around the perimeter.

Pizza omelette

For a quickly made nourishing and satisfying dish, this flat type omelette takes some beating.

Cooking time 3–4 minutes. *Serves* 1

IMPERIAL	AMERICAN
1 oz. ham or bacon, cooked (optional)	2 tablespoons cooked ham or bacon (optional)
1 medium tomato	1 medium tomato
1–$1\frac{1}{2}$ oz. Gruyère, Emmenthal, Cheddar or cheese slices	1–$1\frac{1}{2}$ oz. Gruyère, Emmenthal, Cheddar or cheese slices
2 eggs	2 eggs
1 tablespoon cold water	1 tablespoon cold water
salt, pepper	salt, pepper
$\frac{1}{4}$–$\frac{1}{2}$ oz. butter	$\frac{1}{2}$–1 tablespoon butter
oregano, marjoram or mixed herbs	oregano, marjoram or mixed herbs

Dice the ham or bacon if used. Slice the tomato and the cheese thinly. Break the eggs into a basin, add the water, season with salt and pepper and beat lightly with a fork.

Heat a $5\frac{1}{2}$–6-inch base frying pan, add the butter and move the pan around to allow the butter to spread over the bottom and up the sides a little. When the butter starts to sizzle, pour in the eggs. Stir them lightly and, when they begin to set around the edges, lift to allow the surplus liquid to run underneath. While the centre is still runny, remove the pan from the heat, sprinkle over the chopped ham if used, then the herbs. Arrange the slices of tomato over the top and lastly the cheese.

Place under a hot grill until the cheese is bubbly and just beginning to brown.

Caved eggs

Cooking time 14–16 minutes. Serves 4
Oven temperature 375° F., 190° C., Gas Mark 5

IMPERIAL	AMERICAN
4 crisp, round bread rolls	4 crisp, round bread rolls
$\frac{1}{2}$–$\frac{3}{4}$ tablespoon chopped fresh chives, savory and chervil or half quantity dried savory, chervil, basil or marjoram	$\frac{1}{2}$–$\frac{3}{4}$ tablespoon chopped fresh chives, savory, and chervil or half quantity dried savory, chervil, basil, or marjoram
4 oz. cheese spread	$\frac{1}{2}$ cup cheese spread
salt, pepper	salt, pepper
4 eggs	4 eggs
butter	butter

Cut a slice off the bottom of each roll and scoop out all the soft crumb inside.

Work the herbs into the cheese spread and season with salt and pepper. Line the inside of each roll with the cheese. Break an egg into each, top with flakes of butter and bake in a moderate oven for 14–16 minutes, until the eggs are set.

Savoury egg pie

Cooking time 25–30 minutes. Serves 4
Oven temperature 400° F., 200° C., Gas Mark 6

IMPERIAL	AMERICAN
8 oz. short pastry (made with 8 oz. flour, etc.)	basic pie dough (made with 2 cups flour, etc.)
4 hard-boiled eggs	4 hard-cooked eggs
1 oz. butter	2 tablespoons butter
1 oz. flour	$\frac{1}{4}$ cup all-purpose flour
1$\frac{1}{2}$ teaspoons curry powder	1$\frac{1}{2}$ teaspoons curry powder
7 fl. oz. milk	$\frac{3}{4}$ cup milk
1 tablespoon finely chopped pickle	1 tablespoon finely chopped pickle or relish
salt	salt

Roll out half the dough on a floured board and line a 7-inch flan tin or ring with it.

Cut the eggs in halves lengthways and lay them flat on the pastry, radiating from the centre. Melt the butter, blend in the flour and curry powder. Add the milk and stir with a wire whisk until it boils. Boil for a minute or two, remove from the heat, stir in the pickle and season with salt as necessary. Pour over the eggs and leave until cold before covering.

Roll out the rest of the dough. Moisten the edge of the crust with cold water and cover the flan with the second piece, pressing the two edges together to stick firmly. Trim the edge and decorate the rim by marking with a knife handle. Prick the top with a fork, brush with milk and bake in a moderately hot oven for 25–30 minutes, until nicely browned. Serve hot or cold.

Sweets

Ginger sponge pudding

Cooking time 1$\frac{1}{2}$–1$\frac{3}{4}$ hours. Serves 4–5

IMPERIAL	AMERICAN
3 oz. butter	6 tablespoons butter
2 oz. sugar	$\frac{1}{4}$ cup sugar
1 egg	1 egg
1$\frac{1}{2}$ tablespoons golden syrup	2 tablespoons corn or maple sirup
5 oz. self-raising flour	1$\frac{1}{4}$ cups all-purpose flour, sifted with 1$\frac{1}{4}$ teaspoons double-acting baking powder
2 teaspoons ground ginger	2 teaspoons ground ginger
$\frac{1}{8}$ teaspoon salt	$\frac{1}{8}$ teaspoon salt

Beat the butter and sugar together until light coloured and fluffy. Beat in the egg, golden syrup and lastly the flour, sifted with the ginger and salt. Turn into a greased and floured 2-pint (U.S. 2$\frac{1}{2}$-pint) pudding basin. Cover with foil, twisting it under the rim (or use a basin with its own lid) and steam for 1$\frac{1}{2}$–1$\frac{3}{4}$ hours.

Serve with warm golden syrup diluted with a little water, if liked.

Bilberry pie

Cooking time 25–30 minutes. Serves 4–5
Oven temperature 400° F., 200° C., Gas Mark 6

IMPERIAL	AMERICAN
8 oz. rich short pastry (made from 8 oz. flour, etc.)	rich egg pie dough (made from 2 cups flour, etc.)
1 lb. bilberries	1 lb. blueberries
4–5 oz. sugar	$\frac{1}{2}$ cup plus 2 tablespoons sugar
$\frac{1}{2}$ teaspoon ground cinnamon	$\frac{1}{2}$ teaspoon ground cinnamon

Roll out half the dough on a floured board and line an 8–9-inch pie plate with it. Spread over the washed bilberries mixed with the sugar and cinnamon. Roll out the rest of the dough. Moisten the two edges with cold water and place the second piece on top, pressing the edges well together to stick firmly. Trim around the edge. Brush the top with beaten egg or milk, sprinkle with castor sugar if liked. Cut 3 or 4 slits to allow the steam to escape and bake in a moderately hot oven for 25–30 minutes until golden brown. Serve with cream or custard.

Summer Christmas pudding

This is a lovely Australian recipe and most appropriate since the 25th December is in the middle of the Australian summer. It makes a splendid party piece at any time of the year.

Cooking time 4–5 minutes. *Serves* 5–6

IMPERIAL	AMERICAN
10 oz. mixed dried fruit	scant 2 cups mixed dried fruit
1 teaspoon mixed spice	1 teaspoon mixed spice
¼ teaspoon ground ginger	¼ teaspoon ground ginger
¼ teaspoon grated nutmeg	¼ teaspoon grated nutmeg
2 oz. sugar	¼ cup sugar
1 tablespoon chocolate powder	1 tablespoon sweetened cocoa powder
¾ pint water	2 cups water
5 fl. oz. bottled orange juice	⅔ cup bottled orange juice
½ oz. gelatine	2 envelopes gelatin
3 oz. chopped mixed peel	½ cup chopped, mixed candied peel
3 teaspoons sweet sherry	3 teaspoons sweet sherry
5–10 fl. oz. double cream (optional)	⅔–1¼ cups whipping cream (optional)
toasted almonds (optional)	toasted almonds (optional)

Turn the fruit with the spices, sugar and chocolate powder into a saucepan with the water and orange juice. Bring to the boil and boil for 4–5 minutes until the fruit is soft and plumped up. Remove and stir in the gelatine, previously dissolved in a little very hot water. Mix in the chopped peel and the sherry and turn into a 7½-inch ring mould rinsed out with cold water. Leave to set. Turn out, fill the centre hole with lightly whipped cream. Decorate all round with piped rosettes of cream with a toasted almond stuck into each, if desired. Or decorate with sprigs of holly.

VARIATION: Use ½ pint (U.S. 1¼ cups) Guinness in place of ½ pint (U.S. 1¼ cups) of water and the sherry.

Spicy cream pancakes

Pancakes can be made a day or two ahead and kept with a piece of foil or greaseproof paper between each, then all of them wrapped in the same paper, foil or a cloth. They keep best in a refrigerator.

Cooking time 16–18 minutes. *Makes* 8

Pancakes

IMPERIAL	AMERICAN
4 oz. plain flour	1 cup all-purpose flour
⅛ teaspoon salt	⅛ teaspoon salt
1 large or 2 small eggs	1 large or 2 small eggs
about ½ pint milk and cold water, mixed	about 1¼ cups milk and cold water, mixed

Sieve the flour and salt into a basin. Make a well in the centre and break in the eggs. Pour some of the liquid on to them and gradually stir in the flour by drawing it in from the sides. Whisk with a wire whisk, adding sufficient liquid to make the batter the consistency of thin cream. Leave aside for 30 minutes or more, then give it another whisk before frying, and turn it into a jug (to make it easy for pouring).

TO FRY: Fry in oil. It simplifies the proceedings to have the oil in a jug also. Pour in just enough oil to grease a small (6–7-inch) frying pan. When it is hot, pour in only just sufficient batter to cover thinly the bottom of the frying pan. Cook quickly until the underside is a pale golden brown, lift with a spatula adding a spot more oil. Turn over the pancake and cook other side also. Or toss if preferred.

Filling

Fills 8 pancakes

IMPERIAL	AMERICAN
2 oz. sultanas	⅓ cup seedless white raisins
2 tablespoons cream castor sugar	3 tablespoons cream granulated sugar
8 oz. curd cheese	1 cup curd cheese
about ½ teaspoon ground cinnamon	about ½ teaspoon ground cinnamon

Soak the sultanas for an hour or so in warm water to plump them up, then drain.
Mix the cream, 2 tablespoons (U.S. 3 tablespoons) sugar and enough cinnamon into the cheese to give it a spicy flavour. Stir in sultanas and place spoonfuls along the centre of each pancake. Roll up, place in a shallow heatproof dish, cover with foil and heat through gently in the oven. Sprinkle with more sugar to serve.

Steamed date pudding

Cooking time 2½ hours. Serves 4–5

IMPERIAL	AMERICAN
8 oz. stoned dates	1¼ cups pitted dates
2 oz. self-raising flour	½ cup all-purpose flour, sifted with ½ teaspoon double-acting baking powder
2 oz. soft breadcrumbs	1 cup soft bread crumbs
2 oz. soft brown sugar	¼ cup (firmly packed) soft brown sugar
3 oz. shredded suet	generous ½ cup shredded suet
⅛ teaspoon salt	⅛ teaspoon salt
¼ teaspoon ground ginger	¼ teaspoon ground ginger
¼ teaspoon ground cinnamon	¼ teaspoon ground cinnamon
1 tablespoon brandy or sherry	1 tablespoon brandy or sherry
2 tablespoons milk	3 tablespoons milk
1 egg	1 egg

Chop the dates into fairly small pieces. Mix all the dry ingredients together. Beat the brandy or sherry and milk with the egg and stir into the dry ingredients. Turn into a greased and floured 2-pint (U.S. 2½-pint) pudding basin, tie down with greaseproof paper or twist foil under the rim. Steam for 2½ hours. Turn out on to dish and serve with golden syrup sauce, custard or cream, if liked.

Stewed plums

Plums can be stewed more quickly in a saucepan on top of the cooker, but they tend to burst their skins and look untidy. The cinnamon is especially good with tart plums as it makes the flavour blander and smoother.

Cooking time 28–35 minutes. Serves 4
Oven temperature 325°–350° F., 170°–180° C., Gas Mark 3–4

IMPERIAL	AMERICAN
6 oz. granulated sugar	¾ cup sugar
½ teaspoon ground cinnamon	½ teaspoon ground cinnamon
4 tablespoons water	5 tablespoons water
1½ lb. plums	1½ lb. plums

Melt the sugar and cinnamon in the water in a covered casserole in the oven. Add the washed fruit and bake in a very moderate oven for 20–25 minutes, or until the plums are just tender, turning them over carefully once or twice.

Melons Alaska

(illustrated in colour on page 61)

The flavour of coriander makes this dish mysteriously intriguing.
For anyone with a freezer or freezer compartment, an alternative to ice cream is a lemon sorbet – very refreshing on a warm evening.

Cooking time 3–4 minutes. Serves 4
Oven temperature 450° F., 230° C., Gas Mark 8

IMPERIAL	AMERICAN
2 Charentais or Ogen melons	2 Charentais, Ogen or similar melons
2 large egg whites	2 large egg whites
5 oz. castor sugar	½ cup plus 2 tablespoons granulated sugar
¼–½ teaspoon ground coriander	¼–½ teaspoon ground coriander
1 block chocolate and orange or vanilla ice cream	1 quart chocolate and orange or vanilla ice cream
2 tablespoons Grand Marnier or Curaçao	3 tablespoons Grand Marnier or Curaçao
32–36 halved, blanched almonds	32–36 halved, blanched almonds

Cut the melons in halves horizontally and scoop out all the seeds. Whip the egg whites with a little of the sugar, adding the rest gradually with coriander to taste, until they are stiff enough to stand up in peaks. Place a good portion of the ice cream into the centre of each melon half, pour ½ tablespoon or more of Grand Marnier over each. Cover completely to the skin with the meringue, making sure there are no holes anywhere. Stick 8 or 9 almond halves into each and bake in a hot oven for 3–4 minutes, until the meringue and almonds are lightly browned. Serve immediately.

Vanilla soufflé

Cooking time 28–34 minutes. Serves 4
Oven temperature 350°–375° F., 180°–190° C., Gas Mark 4–5

IMPERIAL	AMERICAN
1½ oz. butter	3 tablespoons butter
1½ oz. plain flour	6 tablespoons all-purpose flour
7½ fl. oz. milk, heated	1 cup milk, heated
2 oz. vanilla sugar, or castor sugar and ⅛ teaspoon vanilla essence	¼ cup vanilla sugar, or granulated sugar and ⅛ teaspoon vanilla extract
4 eggs	4 eggs
1 egg white extra	1 egg white extra

Melt 1 oz. (U.S. 2 tablespoons) of the butter in a largish saucepan. Blend in the flour, add the hot milk gradually, stirring with a wooden spoon until the

mixture leaves the sides of the pan. Remove, beat in the sugar and the rest of the butter until perfectly smooth. Beat in the egg yolks one after the other.
Whip the egg whites stiffly and fold into the panada with a metal spoon. Turn at once into a greased and sugared 7½-inch soufflé dish and bake in a moderate to moderately hot oven for 25–30 minutes, until well risen and golden brown on top.

VARIATIONS: a) Melt 2 oz. (U.S. ⅓ cup) plain chocolate in the milk before using it for making the panada. b) Use half milk and half strong coffee.
c) Add ½ sherry glass Grand Marnier to the panada. When serving the soufflé, pour a little Grand Marnier on to each plate. This causes the aroma to rise excitingly (a French tip!).

Date and orange flan

(illustrated in colour on page 61)

Cooking time 7–10 minutes. Serves 4

IMPERIAL	AMERICAN
6 oz. stoned dates	about 1 cup pitted dates
4 tablespoons stout	5 tablespoons dark beer
¼ teaspoon ground cinnamon	¼ teaspoon ground cinnamon
¼ teaspoon ground cardamom	¼ teaspoon ground cardamom
2 oranges	2 oranges
baked 7-inch short pastry flan case	baked 7-inch pie shell

Chop the dates roughly and boil with the stout and spices until they are the consistency of thick jam, 5–7 minutes. Grate the peel of one orange finely and peel the other. Cut the flesh of both into thin slices and, with a pair of scissors, cut around each slice to remove all the pith.
Spread the date mixture in the flan case, arrange overlapping slices of orange in a circle on top. Place a piece of crystallized violet or glacé cherry in the centre of each slice, if liked. Pour over the syrup and allow it to set to form a glaze.

Syrup

1½ teaspoons arrowroot or cornflour	1½ teaspoons arrowroot or cornstarch
5 fl. oz. water	⅔ cup water
3 oz. granulated sugar	6 tablespoons sugar
grated rind 1 orange	grated rind 1 orange

Make the arrowroot or cornflour into a smooth paste with a little of the water. Bring the rest of the water to the boil, with the sugar and orange, stir and add the paste. Boil for 2–3 minutes until clear. Allow to cool before pouring over the flan.

Floating islands

Cooking time 8–10 minutes or 11–13 minutes. Serves 4–5
Oven temperature (for alternative) 470°–475° F., 240° C., Gas Mark 9

IMPERIAL	AMERICAN
2 large eggs	2 eggs
1 pint milk	2½ cups milk
5 oz. vanilla sugar or castor sugar with vanilla essence	½ cup plus 2 tablespoons vanilla sugar or granulated sugar with vanilla extract

Separate yolks and whites of eggs. Make a custard with the milk, egg yolks and 2 oz. (U.S. ¼ cup) of the sugar. Remove from the heat and if plain castor sugar is used, add ¼ teaspoon vanilla essence or more to taste. Stir occasionally until cool, to prevent a skin forming on the top. Pour into a large shallow dish.
Whip the egg whites adding the sugar gradually (with a little vanilla essence if plain sugar is used), until they are stiff. Place in mounds on top of the custard. Chill.
Decorate with chopped glacé cherries and angelica, if desired.

ALTERNATIVE: Turn the custard into a shallow heatproof dish, scoop the 'islands' on top in the same manner. Place in a very hot oven for about 3 minutes until the 'islands' are lightly browned at the edges.

Rebanades

This is an old traditional Portuguese sweet which used to be made with honey, before sugar was known, but is now more often made with sugar.

Cooking time 4–5 minutes. Serves 4

IMPERIAL	AMERICAN
4 thick slices of bread from a large loaf	4 thick slices of bread from a large loaf
1 egg	1 egg
⅛ teaspoon salt	⅛ teaspoon salt
5 fl. oz. milk	⅔ cup milk
olive oil	olive oil
castor sugar or honey	granulated sugar or honey
ground cinnamon	ground cinnamon

Cut off the crusts from the bread and cut the slices into triangles or squares. Beat the egg with the salt and then beat in the milk. Soak the bread in the mixture for 1–2 minutes. Fry in deep hot oil (350°–370° F., 180°–185° C.), or in a frying pan until golden brown on both sides. Drain and serve hot, sprinkled with sugar or honey and liberally with cinnamon.

Apple charlotte

Cooking time 35–42 minutes. Serves 4–5
Oven temperature 425°–450° F., 220°–230° C., Gas Mark 7–8

IMPERIAL	AMERICAN
1½ lb. cooking apples, after peeling and coring	1½ lb. baking apples, after peeling and coring
3 oz. granulated sugar	6 tablespoons sugar
juice ½ lemon	juice ½ lemon
4 cloves	4 cloves
½ teaspoon ground cinnamon	½ teaspoon ground cinnamon
1–2 tablespoons sultanas (optional)	1–3 tablespoons seedless white raisins (optional)
4 thin slices buttered bread (from a large loaf)	4 thin slices buttered bread (from a large loaf)
2 oz. soft breadcrumbs	1 cup soft bread crumbs
soft brown sugar	soft brown sugar
butter	butter

Stew the apples with the granulated sugar, lemon juice, cloves, cinnamon and sultanas, if used, until the apples are soft and pulpy, 5–8 minutes. Roughly squash them with a fork.

Line the bottom and sides of a 2¾-pint (U.S. 3½-pint) pie dish with the bread slices, buttered side outwards. Pour the apple into the centre, scatter over the breadcrumbs, sprinkle thickly with soft brown sugar. Dot with flakes of butter and bake above centre in a hot to very hot oven for 30–35 minutes, until the sugar has melted and the top is crunchy.

Sagou à la plaza

I learned this simple sweet at one of the smartest hotels on the French Riviera and it has been a favourite with the family ever since.

Cooking time 15–20 minutes. Serves 4

IMPERIAL	AMERICAN
1½ pints milk (some single cream makes it extra delicious)	3¾ cups milk (some coffee cream makes it extra delicious)
1 vanilla pod	1 vanilla bean
2 oz. sago	scant ¼ cup sago
2 oz. castor sugar	¼ cup sugar
1 egg yolk	1 egg yolk
3 fl. oz. double cream	about ½ cup whipping cream
4 glacé cherries	4 candied cherries

Bring the milk to the boil with the vanilla pod in it. Scatter in the sago and boil, stirring, until every grain is transparent, 15–20 minutes. Remove from the heat and take out the vanilla pod. Beat in the sugar and egg yolk. Stir occasionally while it cools to prevent a skin forming, then pour into 4 glasses and chill. Decorate with a rosette or blob of lightly whipped cream and a glacé cherry.

VARIATION: Chopped glacé fruit may be mixed into the sago after the sugar and egg yolk have been beaten in.

Bread, Biscuits and Cakes

Feather gingerbread

Intriguing to make because when the mixture is poured into the tin it is just like thick sauce! The result is a soft light cake which will keep in a cake box for at least two weeks without getting dry.

Cooking time 40–45 minutes
Oven temperature 350° F., 180° C., Gas Mark 4
Size of tin: 11½ by 9 inches (across the top) roasting tin
Preparation of tin: brush with oil and line with grease-proof

IMPERIAL	AMERICAN
6 oz. butter	¾ cup butter
5 oz. soft brown sugar	½ cup plus 2 tablespoons (firmly packed) soft brown sugar
8 oz. black treacle	⅔ cup molasses
2 eggs	2 eggs
9 oz. self-raising flour	2¼ cups all-purpose flour, sifted with 2½ teaspoons double-acting baking powder
½ teaspoon bicarbonate of soda	½ teaspoon baking soda
½ tablespoon ground ginger	½ tablespoon ground ginger
1 teaspoon ground cinnamon	1 teaspoon ground cinnamon
¼ teaspoon ground cloves	¼ teaspoon ground cloves
½ teaspoon grated nutmeg	½ teaspoon grated nutmeg
4 fl. oz. Guinness stout or milk	½ cup dark beer or milk
4 fl. oz. water	½ cup water
ginger butter icing	ginger butter icing
preserved ginger	preserved ginger

Melt the butter and mix with the sugar and treacle. Stir in the beaten eggs until well blended. Sift the flour with the rest of the dry ingredients and beat into the butter mixture. Stir in the boiling Guinness and water and pour into the prepared tin. Bake in a moderate oven for 40–45 minutes. Leave in the tin until cool before turning out on to a wire cake rack. Spread ginger butter icing over the top and smooth with a spatula or knife dipped into warm water.

Decorate with thin slices of preserved ginger, arranged in the shape of a flower in the centre and petals at the corners. Sprinkle finely chopped ginger round the edge.

Ginger butter icing

IMPERIAL	AMERICAN
4 oz. butter	$\frac{1}{2}$ cup butter
8 oz. icing sugar	scant 2 cups sifted confectioners' sugar
1–2 tablespoons ginger syrup	1–3 tablespoons ginger sirup
ginger essence	ginger extract

Cream the butter well, add the sieved sugar and continue beating until the mixture is smooth and creamy. Gradually beat in ginger syrup and essence to give flavour and make icing soft enough to spread.

Speculaas

Always served on St. Nicholas Eve (5th December) in Holland, these are a special Dutch biscuit.

Cooking time 10–13 minutes. *Makes 25–27 round biscuits*
Oven temperature 375° F., 190° C., Gas Mark 5

IMPERIAL	AMERICAN
8 oz. self-raising flour	2 cups all-purpose flour, sifted with 2$\frac{1}{4}$ teaspoons double-acting baking powder
$\frac{1}{8}$ teaspoon salt	$\frac{1}{8}$ teaspoon salt
1 teaspoon ground cinnamon	1 teaspoon ground cinnamon
$\frac{1}{2}$ teaspoon ground mixed spice	$\frac{1}{2}$ teaspoon ground mixed spice
6 oz. butter	$\frac{3}{4}$ cup butter
5 oz. soft light brown sugar	$\frac{1}{2}$ cup plus 2 tablespoons (firmly packed) soft light brown sugar
grated rind $\frac{1}{2}$ lemon	grated rind $\frac{1}{2}$ lemon
4 oz. ground almonds	1 cup ground almonds
1 oz. shortbread biscuits, crushed	$\frac{1}{4}$ cup crushed shortbread cookies
flaked almonds (optional)	flaked almonds (optional)

Sieve the flour, salt and spices together. Cream the butter and sugar until light and fluffy. Beat in the lemon rind, then work in the ground almonds, biscuit crumbs and flour. Knead until smooth. Roll out on a floured board to less than $\frac{1}{4}$ inch in thickness and cut into animal, little men or heart shapes, or into rounds with a 2$\frac{1}{2}$-inch cutter. Flaked almonds may be scattered over the top and lightly pressed in, if liked. Bake on trays in a moderate oven for 10–13 minutes until lightly coloured. Remove with a spatula and cool on a wire cake rack.

Ginger shortbread biscuits

These biscuits were my father's favourites and he was seldom without some in stock. The amount of ginger can be varied according to the strength of the powder and the heat preferred by individual taste.

Cooking time 25–30 minutes. *Makes 30–33 biscuits*
Oven temperature 375° F., 190° C., Gas Mark 5

IMPERIAL	AMERICAN
1$\frac{1}{4}$ oz. ground ginger	1$\frac{1}{4}$ oz. ground ginger
12 oz. plain flour	3 cups all-purpose flour
6 oz. castor sugar	$\frac{3}{4}$ cup granulated sugar
9 oz. butter	1 cup plus 2 tablespoons butter

Sieve the ginger into the flour, stir in the sugar and rub in the butter. Knead until smooth.
Turn out on to a floured board and roll out to less than $\frac{1}{4}$ inch in thickness. Cut into circles with a 2$\frac{1}{4}$-inch pastry cutter. Place on baking trays and bake until very lightly coloured only.

Banana bread

Cooking time 55–60 minutes
Oven temperature 350° F., 180° C., Gas Mark 4
Size of tin: 9 by 5 by 2$\frac{1}{2}$ inches loaf tin
Preparation of tin: brush with oil

IMPERIAL	AMERICAN
10 oz. self-raising flour	2$\frac{1}{2}$ cups all-purpose flour, sifted with 2$\frac{3}{4}$ teaspoons double-acting baking powder
$\frac{1}{2}$ teaspoon bicarbonate of soda	$\frac{1}{2}$ teaspoon baking soda
$\frac{1}{4}$ teaspoon salt	$\frac{1}{4}$ teaspoon salt
$\frac{1}{4}$ teaspoon ground cardamom	$\frac{1}{4}$ teaspoon ground cardamom
$\frac{1}{4}$ teaspoon ground mace	$\frac{1}{4}$ teaspoon ground mace
4 oz. butter	$\frac{1}{2}$ cup butter
6 oz. castor sugar	$\frac{3}{4}$ cup granulated sugar
2 eggs	2 eggs
$\frac{1}{4}$ teaspoon vanilla essence	$\frac{1}{4}$ teaspoon vanilla extract
4 oz. (about 3 bananas) banana, mashed	1 cup mashed banana
3 oz. walnuts, chopped	$\frac{3}{4}$ cup chopped walnuts

Sift together the flour, bicarbonate of soda, salt and spices. Cream the butter and sugar until light and beat in the eggs and vanilla essence gradually. Stir in the flour and banana alternately and lastly the nuts.
Turn into the prepared tin, level the top and bake in a moderate oven for 55–60 minutes. Leave in the tin until cool, before turning out. Serve cut into slices and buttered.

Herb bread

This bread is delicious with many dishes and for a party. The herbs can be varied, such as parsley, chives, a little rosemary, lemon thyme. Or parsley, chives, and fennel or dill for serving with fish.

Cooking time 15–18 minutes. *Serves 4–5 greedy people!*
Oven temperature 425° F., 220° C., Gas Mark 7

IMPERIAL	AMERICAN
1 tablespoon (pressed down) chopped fresh herbs – parsley, chives (plenty), marjoram, thyme, chervil (optional)	1 tablespoon (firmly packed) chopped fresh herbs – parsley, chives (plenty), marjoram, thyme, chervil (optional)
2½ oz. salted butter	5 tablespoons salted butter
1 (13–15-inch) French loaf	1 (13–15-inch) French loaf

Mix the herbs thoroughly into the softened butter. Cut the loaf into diagonal ½-inch slices, but not quite through, and spread each slice with some of the butter. Press the loaf together again and wrap in foil. Place in a hot oven for 15–18 minutes.

VARIATION: For Garlic bread, put one large or two cloves of garlic through a garlic press, or chop finely and crush with a knife, then cream into the butter and treat as for Herb bread.

Poppy seed cocktailers

Little biscuits are ideal for serving with drinks of any kind. These will keep for weeks in an airtight container, and indefinitely in a freezer.

Cooking time 12–15 minutes. *Makes about 9½ dozen*
Oven temperature 400° F., 200° C., Gas Mark 6

IMPERIAL	AMERICAN
3 oz. poppy seeds	scant ½ cup poppy seeds
4½ oz. plain flour	1 cup plus 2 tablespoons all-purpose flour
½ teaspoon salt	½ teaspoon salt
scant ⅛ teaspoon cayenne pepper	scant ⅛ teaspoon cayenne pepper
2½ oz. butter and lard mixed	5 tablespoons butter and lard mixed
cold water	cold water

Turn the seeds on to a baking tray and bake in a moderately hot oven for 15–20 minutes. Allow to get quite cold, then mix with all the dry ingredients in a bowl. Rub in the fats and stir in just sufficient cold water to make the dough bind. Turn on to a floured board and roll out very thinly. Cut into circles with a 1½-inch fluted pastry cutter. Place on baking trays and bake in a moderately hot oven for 12–15 minutes, or before they turn brown. Sprinkle with salt before removing if liked.

Simnel cake

A Simnel cake is most often served on Easter Sunday, but it should be made for Mothering Sunday.

Cooking time 2¾ hours
Oven temperature 350° F., 180° C., Gas Mark 4 and 320° F., 170° C., Gas Mark 3. *Size of tin:* 8-inch cake tin
Preparation of tin: brush with oil and line with greaseproof

IMPERIAL	AMERICAN
8 oz. butter	2 cups butter
8 oz. castor sugar	generous 1 cup sugar
3 large eggs	3 large eggs
10 oz. self-raising flour	2½ cups all-purpose flour, sifted with 2¾ teaspoons baking powder
¾ teaspoon mixed spice	¾ teaspoon mixed spice
½ teaspoon grated nutmeg	½ teaspoon grated nutmeg
¼ teaspoon salt	¼ teaspoon salt
8 oz. currants	1⅓ cups currants
6 oz. seedless raisins	1 cup seedless raisins
3 oz. sultanas	½ cup seedless white raisins
4 oz. chopped mixed peel	⅔ cup chopped, mixed candied peel
3 oz. glacé cherries, cut in halves (optional)	scant ⅓ cup candied cherries, cut in halves (optional)
almond paste	almond paste
apricot jam	apricot jam

Cream the butter and sugar until light and fluffy. Beat in each egg separately. Sieve all the dry ingredients together and stir into the creamed mixture. Add the fruit and turn half the mixture into the prepared tin. Place a circle of almond paste on top, then cover with the rest of the cake mixture. Bake in a moderate oven for 45 minutes, then lower the heat to very moderate and continue baking for a further 2 hours. Leave in the tin until cool before turning out. When quite cold, turn upside-down and spread lightly with sieved apricot jam. Cover the top with the second circle of almond paste, smooth it evenly and trim the sides. Roll the rest of the paste into 12 small balls (one for each of the Disciples) and place them around outside edge. Brown lightly under grill.

Almond paste

12 oz. ground almonds	3 cups ground almonds
6 oz. castor sugar	¾ cup granulated sugar
6 oz. icing sugar	1½ cups sifted confectioners' sugar
1 small egg, 1 egg yolk	1 small egg, 1 egg yolk
¼ teaspoon almond essence	¼ teaspoon almond extract

Mix together the almonds and sieved sugars. Make a well in the centre and add the lightly beaten egg and egg yolk with the essence, working into the dry ingredients and kneading thoroughly. Cut into three portions (two larger than the third). Roll out the larger pieces into 8-inch circles, use the rest for decoration.

Drinks

Mint tea

Peppermint or spearmint can be used for this tea. The former is said to be superior for flavour, but it depends upon individual taste.

The quantity of mint also depends upon the strength of flavour desired. I have given the quantity I prefer. Other herbs for tea may be treated in exactly the same way.

Makes 4 teacups

IMPERIAL	AMERICAN
7–8 tablespoons mint, chopped or torn into little pieces (use more or less according to taste and time of year)	$\frac{1}{2}$–$\frac{2}{3}$ cup mint, chopped or torn into little pieces (use more or less according to taste and time of year)
1 pint boiling water	2$\frac{1}{2}$ cups boiling water
sugar or honey	sugar or honey

Turn the mint into a china or earthenware teapot. Pour over the boiling water and leave to infuse for 5 minutes. Strain to serve.
Sweeten with sugar or honey. A little lemon juice or a slice of lemon may also be added.

Port Negus

Florence Nightingale is said to have given Port Negus as a health-giving drink to the sick and wounded in the Crimea.

Serves 4–5

IMPERIAL	AMERICAN
1 pint port	2$\frac{1}{2}$ cups port
3-inch stick cinnamon	3-inch stick cinnamon
$\frac{1}{4}$ teaspoon grated nutmeg	$\frac{1}{4}$ teaspoon grated nutmeg
$\frac{1}{2}$ tablespoon sugar	$\frac{1}{2}$ tablespoon sugar
$\frac{1}{4}$ pint water, boiling	$\frac{2}{3}$ cup boiling water

Heat the port with the cinnamon stick, nutmeg and sugar, but do not allow it to boil. Pour in the boiling water, remove the cinnamon and serve.

Mulled ale

Mulled ale was a very popular tipple in England in the 18th and 19th centuries and deserves a return to popularity. It is an excellent pick-you-up for invalids and influenza-weary patients, or anybody wanting a warm-up.

Serves 3

IMPERIAL	AMERICAN
1 pint (mild) ale	2$\frac{1}{2}$ cups beer
1 egg	1 egg
$\frac{1}{2}$ tablespoon sugar	$\frac{1}{2}$ tablespoon sugar
$\frac{1}{4}$ teaspoon ground mace	$\frac{1}{4}$ teaspoon ground mace
$\frac{1}{4}$ teaspoon ground nutmeg	$\frac{1}{4}$ teaspoon ground nutmeg

Stir a bare half cup of the ale into the beaten egg. Bring the rest of the ingredients to the boil, remove and allow to cool. Whip in the egg mixture and heat through *without* allowing it to boil (or the mixture will curdle).

Burgundy wine cup

A delicious cool drink for a summer's day.

Serves 10–12

IMPERIAL	AMERICAN
2 bottles Burgundy	2 bottles Burgundy
$\frac{1}{2}$ pint dry sherry	1$\frac{1}{4}$ cups dry sherry
$\frac{1}{4}$ pint Chartreuse, Cointreau or Curacao (optional)	$\frac{2}{3}$ cup Chartreuse, Cointreau, or Curacao (optional)
juice 3–4 oranges or 6–7 fl. oz. bottled orange, strained	juice 3–4 oranges, or $\frac{2}{3}$–1 cup concentrated orange drink, strained
juice 2 lemons	juice 2 lemons
2 tablespoons sugar (omit if bottled orange is used)	3 tablespoons sugar (omit if bottled orange is used)
strips cucumber peel	strips cucumber peel
$\frac{1}{2}$ pint port	1$\frac{1}{4}$ cups port
2 syphons soda water	2 syphons soda water
8–12 oz. fresh fruit in season – strawberries, cherries, peaches, pears, apples	$\frac{1}{2}$–$\frac{3}{4}$ lb. fresh fruit in season – strawberries, cherries, peaches, pears, apples
sprigs borage and/or lemon thyme	sprigs borage and/or lemon thyme

In a bowl, mix the Burgundy, sherry, liqueur if used, orange and lemon juice, sugar, and strips of cucumber. Chill.
Just before the guests arrive mix in the port and soda water. Place whole small fruit or sliced larger fruit in the bottom of the requisite number of jugs. Pour in the liquid and distribute the cucumber equally. Float sprigs of the herbs on top of each jug.

Mulled cider

In the United States, 'cider' usually means pure apple juice with no alcoholic content. This is an American recipe and therefore is non-alcoholic, but ordinary cider may be used in place of the pure apple juice. And if a stronger drink is desired, there is nothing nicer to my mind than vintage apple wine.

Cooking time 10 minutes. Enough for 6 ¼-pint glasses

IMPERIAL	AMERICAN
2½ oz. soft brown sugar	5 tablespoons (firmly packed) soft brown sugar
⅛ teaspoon salt	⅛ teaspoon salt
¼ teaspoon ground cloves	¼ teaspoon ground cloves
¼ teaspoon ground allspice	¼ teaspoon ground allspice
⅛ teaspoon grated nutmeg	⅛ teaspoon grated nutmeg
1-inch stick cinnamon	1-inch stick cinnamon
1 quart bottled apple juice	5 cups bottled apple juice

Mix the sugar, salt, and spices in a saucepan. Stir in the apple juice, bring to the boil and simmer gently for 10 minutes.
Strain through muslin and reheat when required.

Cider cup

For a delicious yet reasonably priced party drink, try this recipe. Make it with vintage apple wine or champagne cider for best results, or with any other cider for a less potent drink.

Serves 12

IMPERIAL	AMERICAN
1 orange	1 orange
1 lemon	1 lemon
1 (12 oz.) can pineapple cubes	1 (12 oz.) can pineapple cubes
½ pint dry or medium sherry	1¼ cups dry or medium sherry
3 (26 fl. oz.) or 4 (20 fl. oz.) bottles cider	approx. 5 pints bottled cider
1 pint soda water	2½ cups soda water
12 Maraschino cherries (optional)	12 Maraschino cherries (optional)
sprigs mint and/or borage	sprigs mint and/or borage

Peel the orange and lemon thinly and turn the peel into a large bowl with the juice of both, the contents of the can of pineapple and the sherry.
Chill.
When ready to serve, pour over the chilled cider and soda water. Pour into jugs and add cherries and a sprig of mint and/or borage to each.

Stuffings, Pickles and Chutneys

Pickled onions

Cooking time 5 minutes. Fills two 2 lb. jam jars

IMPERIAL	AMERICAN
2 lb. pickling (silverskin) onions	2 lb. pickling (silverskin) onions
salt	salt
½ tablespoon mixed pickling spice	½ tablespoon mixed pickling spice
1½ pints vinegar	3¾ cups vinegar
½ tablespoon sugar	½ tablespoon sugar

Sprinkle the peeled onions with salt and leave for several hours or overnight. Rinse off the salt and pat dry the onions. Pack tightly into the jars.
Bring the rest of the ingredients to the boil, stirring until the sugar is dissolved, and boil for 5 minutes. Allow to cool, then strain over the onions. Cover when cold.
Leave for 2–3 months before eating.

Gooseberry stuffing

Cooking time 2–3 minutes. Sufficient for a duck

IMPERIAL	AMERICAN
4–5 oz. gooseberries	approx. ¼ lb. gooseberries
liver 1 duck	liver 1 duck
1 oz. butter	2 tablespoons butter
2½ teaspoons sage	2½ teaspoons sage
¾ teaspoon seasoned salt	¾ teaspoon seasoned salt
good grinding black pepper	freshly cracked black pepper
5 oz. soft breadcrumbs	2½ cups fresh soft bread crumbs

Wash, top and tail the gooseberries and chop them finely. Fry the liver in the butter for 2–3 minutes, then chop into small pieces.
Mix the sage, salt and pepper into the breadcrumbs. Stir in the liver, the butter in which it was fried and the gooseberries.

Pickled eggs

Pickled eggs have been a favourite for snacks in old English country pubs for goodness knows how long, each landlord pickling them to his own recipe.

I have been given recipes which vary from seven parts water to one part vinegar, to all vinegar. This is the strength I prefer, but try any variation to your own taste.

Cooking time 10 minutes

IMPERIAL	AMERICAN
12 medium eggs	12 eggs
dried chillis	dried chili peppers
17 fl. oz. water	generous 2 cups water
6 fl. oz. white malt vinegar	¾ cup white malt vinegar
¾ oz. whole pickling spice, tied in muslin	¾ oz. whole pickling spice, tied in cheese cloth
2-inch piece orange peel	2-inch piece orange peel
1 large clove garlic, cut in half	1 large clove garlic, cut in half

Bring the eggs to the boil in sufficient water to cover them. Boil for 8–10 minutes, without the water boiling so furiously as to risk cracking the shells. Plunge immediately into cold water to prevent a dark rim forming between the yolk and white. Better still, cool under a running cold tap. Shell carefully and pack into bottles. Place one chilli in each bottle.

Bring the rest of the ingredients to the boil and boil for 10 minutes. Allow to get cold. Strain over the eggs to cover them completely. Leave for at least a month before serving.

Sausage and prune stuffing

Cooking time 7–8 minutes. Sufficient for the neck of a turkey or a small chicken

IMPERIAL	AMERICAN
2 oz. prunes, unsoaked	⅓ cup unsoaked prunes
3 oz. onion, finely chopped	¾ cup finely chopped onion
1½ oz. butter	3 tablespoons butter
8 oz. sausage meat	½ lb. sausage meat
2 oz. plain biscuit crumbs	¾ cup cracker crumbs
½ teaspoon mixed herbs	½ teaspoon mixed herbs
¼ teaspoon oregano	¼ teaspoon oregano
1 tablespoon sherry	1 tablespoon sherry
salt, pepper	salt, pepper

Pour boiling water over the prunes and leave them to soak overnight. Drain, remove the stones and cut the flesh into small pieces.

Fry the onion in the butter until golden. Add the sausage meat, biscuit crumbs and herbs, continue frying for 4–5 minutes. Remove from the heat, stir in the prunes and sherry and season with salt and pepper.

Pickled mushrooms

If too strong a flavour of vinegar is not appreciated, dilute the vinegar with water to 25 per cent or 50 per cent.

Cooking time 10–15 minutes. Fills two 12-oz. jars

IMPERIAL	AMERICAN
1 lb. button mushrooms	approx. 4 cups button mushrooms
white malt vinegar	white malt vinegar
2 blades mace	2 blades mace
4 peppercorns, lightly crushed	4 peppercorns, lightly crushed
1 teaspoon ground ginger	1 teaspoon ground ginger
1 teaspoon salt	1 teaspoon salt
½ oz. onion, chopped finely	2 tablespoons finely chopped onion

Wash the mushrooms quickly, trim the stalks and cut any large mushrooms in halves. Turn into a saucepan and just cover with vinegar. Stir in the rest of the ingredients. Bring to the boil, cover the pan and simmer very gently for 10–15 minutes.

Remove the mushrooms with a straining spoon and fill the jars. Strain over enough of the hot vinegar to cover them and seal the jars immediately. Leave for at least 2 weeks before opening.

Harvest chutney

Cooking time 1¼–1½ hours. Makes 7 lb.

IMPERIAL	AMERICAN
2 lb. cooking apples, after peeling and coring	2 lb. baking apples, after peeling and coring
1 lb. onions, peeled	1 lb. onions, peeled
2 lb. plums	2 lb. plums
12 oz. tomatoes (green or red)	¾ lb. tomatoes (green or red)
4 oz. preserved ginger	¼ lb. preserved ginger
12 dried chillis	12 dried chili peppers
1 clove garlic	1 clove garlic
1 lb. seedless raisins	1 lb. seedless raisins
1½ lb. Demerara sugar	1½ lb. brown sugar
2 oz. salt	¼ cup salt
½ teaspoon black pepper	½ teaspoon black pepper
1½ tablespoons ground mixed spice	2 tablespoons ground mixed spice
¾ pint malt vinegar	scant 2 cups malt vinegar

Put the apples and onions through a coarse mincer. Wash and stone the plums and cut into small pieces with the tomatoes (skinned if ripe). Chop finely the ginger, the chillis and garlic. Turn everything into a large pan. Bring to the boil gently, stirring until the sugar is completely dissolved. Boil, stirring occasionally at first and continuously towards the end, for 1¼–1½ hours.

Pour into warm bottles and seal immediately.

NOTE: If a less hot chutney is preferred, omit the ginger and a few of the chillis.

Index